ADAPTIVE

ADAPTIVE

SCALING EMPATHY AND TRUST TO CREATE WORKPLACE NIRVANA

CHRISTOPHER CREEL

LIONCREST
PUBLISHING

ADAPTIVE

Scaling Empathy and Trust to Create Workplace Nirvana

ISBN   978-1-5445-0268-7 *Paperback*
        978-1-5445-0269-4 *Ebook*

I would like to dedicate this book to my daughter, Hannah. I hope Adaptive leads to workplaces that take full advantage of her potential and the potential of her generation and future generations.

CONTENTS

———

FOREWORD

———

I have spent the past twenty-five years working in human resources at both small and large companies, including everywhere from Bank of America to the Coca-Cola company.

In 2007 I left Coca-Cola to work as the head of human resources for a small technology company. We were building our HR practices with a focus on attracting the right talent. However, most of our HR policies were fairly conventional until 2012. It was at that point our company started looking for someone who could lead our technology innovation area.

In walked Chris Creel.

I walked out of my interview with Chris thinking, "This guy is going to break all the rules and turn this place upside down." I wondered if we were ready for Chris, but I also knew we needed to focus more on creating a culture of innovation. The CEO and COO agreed that while Chris may be unconventional, he was probably exactly what we needed.

It seemed reasonable that Chris would break some glass given that we were interviewing him to help us innovate. Little did I know exactly what that would mean in the coming years.

Chris first approached me about his vision of how work should get done and the ways in which our human resource practices could get in the way of that. While our HR policies were business driven and flexible where they could be, Chris pointed out that a hierarchical culture would not support an innovative environment. My response was, "Then go figure out what an innovation culture looks like."

Over a period of months, Chris and I discussed the changes he wanted to make. He created a new employee handbook and started recruiting the kind of people he needed to attract to create that innovative culture. That was just the beginning.

Adaptive is a book about a solution that solves cultural impediments for attracting the right people who want to do their best work in an environment built on trust and empathy.

In the coming pages, you will discover how unleashing the human spirit creates powerful results. The idea that the people doing the work usually know what needs to be done is not revolutionary. However, creating the kind of feedback system that unites teams around the work in real time is unique.

Chris also discovered that human relationships can be augmented with carefully constructed bots that allow the team to focus on solving bigger problems. Here, he demonstrates how bots can be used to provide feedback in a way that supports innovation, the human spirit, and the feedback system, while also building trust and demonstrating empathy.

I was part of the Adaptive Experiment and served as a first-hand witness for both the journey and the amazing results. This book is the result of that experiment. You will be amazed at how much you are about to learn that can be practically applied.

Take the journey!

Valerie Usilton, Human Resources and Leadership Consultant
June 2019

I'M TALKING TO YOU

———

When I started the Adaptive Experiment in 2013, I had a deep sense that the way businesses were being run had begun to falter. I couldn't put my finger on it but felt that a new class of collaboration technologies (such as Slack and HipChat) that had burst onto the scene in 2009 might lead to a new way of thinking about everything we find in everyday business. Frankly, I had no idea what I was getting myself into. Little did I realize the far-reaching implications of this experiment:

- Addressing the vacuum of empathy and trust that destroys corporate potential
- Tackling ineffectual strategy execution plans
- Managing employees, including issues of growth, sustainability, and productively addressing under-performing employees
- Fixing tragically broken annual review processes

- Replacing the constellation of disjointed tools used to solve the problems above
- The impact that chatbots could have on how humans interact with one another, enabling them to be more human and less robotic

What started out as a secondary research project, which gradually evolved into an obsession, then this book, and now a new company. The participants in this experiment became increasingly insistent that I figure out a way to bring Adaptive to the rest of the world. When my CEO said, "We've never seen engagement scores like this," I began to think everyone I was talking to might be on to something. One night over dinner in Asia, my COO said to me, "The impact you've had on people's lives should be what you are most proud of. You can walk away right now and be proud of that for the rest of your life." With that, I realized that despite the billion-dollar return I had helped bring to my company's stakeholders, it was actually Adaptive that was my true calling.

If you are an executive, specifically a chief executive officer, chief human resource executive, chief operating officer, or chief information officer, I suspect that more than one of the implications from the list above piqued your interest. If you are a chief transformation officer, you will soon learn about the most powerful transformation tools that have ever existed and how they are already transforming your business. If you are a servant leader, you should be sitting on the edge of your seat because you are the new hero of the coming age. If you are an individual contributor who feels unmoored in a world of rapid change, this book will be a light in the darkness to show you a better way forward, providing a continuous runway of personal and professional growth, all thanks to a swarm of chatbots.

Regardless of who you are, thank you for reading my book. I am so profoundly grateful that you decided to give me a chance to tell you about this journey. Business has entered a new age without realizing it, and the resulting anxiety is threatening to create unnecessarily destructive cycles. I hope this book will help you understand how to harness these changes as opposed to being subjected to them.

Everything described in this book was done inside of large, highly regulated, and conservative companies. Companies like these typically would have seen my work as heretical. What changed that allowed this work to be possible inside environments that are inherently hostile to change? Here is what I have found: the rapidly changing landscape of technology, workplace demographics, and globalization requires that companies move away from the parochial "unfreeze, change, sustain" model of organizational change. We are moving out of business environments driven by large, episodic changes and into one that demands more fluid and organically continuous change. This is the metaphorical difference between accelerating in a car with a stick shift versus accelerating in one with an electric motor. Ignoring these trends is causing more harm than good as businesses and the people who manage them try to exert control to maintain the status quo instead of harnessing the power of change.

But the sheer complexity of orchestrating all the pieces necessary to achieve continuous strategic change is beyond human capacity. To create sustainable strategic change, you must augment your teams with powerful collaboration tools and bots capable of shouldering the logistical burdens.

You may already have one of these collaboration technologies, like Slack, installed on your phone for personal use. Slack is one of the fastest-growing companies in the world for business collaboration. If your company isn't officially using it, chances are good that there is a team within your company that is quietly using it to work together better. Or maybe your company already has Microsoft Teams, and you just don't know it yet. There are scads of these technologies bursting on to the scene, each one trying to one-up the other. When you see this activity, rest assured that something is indeed afoot.

People naturally gravitate toward collaboration. It is what makes us human. It is collaboration that helped us become the apex species on this planet. The hypercollaboration afforded by these platforms is addictive because it enables us to solve problems *together* quickly, and introverts and extroverts alike derive deep satisfaction from that. Trying to stop these technologies will be like trying to stop water—you will eventually lose. It is better to harness the power of water than try to stop it, and the same is true of these new corporate collaboration tools.

At the time of this writing, bots operating in these collaboration platforms typically have a single focus and are quite rudimentary. That is changing fast, however. The bots I build are sophisticated characters inspired by nonplayer characters (NPC) designed in video games back-ended by powerful artificial intelligence and infrastructure. This new class of powerful chatbots will increasingly take over rote tasks from humans. This rapid evolution will help companies achieve more fluid organizational designs and greater competitive leverage.

You may read this book and think, "This is incredible! Too bad there is no way I could do this at my company." Not true. In fact, *you don't have a choice*. The findings from the Adaptive Experiment are coming to you whether you like it or not. We are in an epic transition that you already feel but can't quite name. New collaboration technologies have strapped booster rockets to this transition. The collaboration technologies I write about in this book are like learning a new word—now that it's in your consciousness, you are about to notice it everywhere. These technologies are creating a new form of hypercollaboration, and we are just starting to scratch the surface.

INTRODUCTION

———

I have a friend who was a crash-site investigator for the Air Force. One day, an F-16 went down. The pilot survived. My friend was sent to help figure out what had gone wrong. Everyone was puzzled; there didn't seem to be a logical explanation. Finally, my friend noticed that a single bolt had not been checked off on the plane's sign-in sheet.

With a little research, he discovered that the maintenance person charged with replacing the bolt had been called away for a family emergency. Distracted, the mechanic handed the bolt to someone else without explaining what needed to be done. That person promptly put the bolt in their pocket without understanding what it was. Several hours later, the plane crashed. All because of a forgotten bolt.

A jet plane crashed because one simple human inter-action disrupted a process that required fast, robotic execution from its participants. One moment of broken collaboration could have gotten someone killed. People are not robots, but a new age is dawning in which humans will be augmented by powerful bots.

This might sound scary to some, but bots and robots will enable humans to be, well, more human. It will allow them to do human things like help a colleague in the moment of a family crisis because the machines can worry about what happened to the bolt that was to be affixed to the jet plane. When you are moving forward at supersonic speed—as we are in the business world today—there is no room for error. Bots and robots have the advantage at speeds like these.

In today's hypercompetitive, rapidly changing environ-ment, running a company is the equivalent of flying an F-16 running on processes that expect robotic execution from flawed humans.

As recently as a few years ago, businesses were driving down the highway in an SUV at 55 miles per hour. At that speed, the tolerance for error is high. If a deer runs out in front of the car, we can slam on the brakes, and everyone will survive (including the deer). If someone swerves into our lane, we can react. If the tire has a loose lug nut, we will probably be all right. None of these things will lead to catastrophic failure.

Today, no one can drive at a reasonable speed. Every business must be an F-16, zooming forward at breakneck speed. The faster we go, the greater the risk. If so much as a bolt is loose, everyone on that plane goes down.

THE BROKEN ORG CHART

The speed of business today requires that we be nimble, quick, and resilient. We must be able to turn on a dime and to use every resource at our fingertips to its maximum advantage. Instead of expecting robotic execution from employees, we should instead augment employees with smart bots to outsource inhuman work. Let humans do what they do best—create and leverage relationships to do creative things. Yet at the core of almost every company lies an ancient, brittle, manually operated device designed to treat humans like cogs in a machine and that ignores our relationships: the org chart.

The trope that "every company's greatest resource is the human beings who work for it" is, I humbly submit, short-sighted. The greatest resource is the invisible web of ever-shifting relationships between people who are trying to get stuff done. Static org charts are a blunt instrument that attempt to describe the components of a machine while completely ignoring its most crucial part: the social network that actually gets stuff done.

Increasingly powerful technologies, rapidly changing workplace demographics, and globalization are tossing companies about like a dingy on an angry ocean, requiring us to collaborate in different ways with an ever-shifting landscape of people. Company org charts simply can't withstand the turbulence, and they've reached a point where they can't reorganize fast enough. Org charts don't allow people, systems, and processes to quickly evolve in ways they need to. Instead, companies look to central planning committees to make omniscient decisions about how it should all work. These committees look at the business like a mechanic might look at a machine, not like a doctor might look at a patient. But people aren't machines, and as a result of expecting them to behave as such, they are miserable, productivity suffers, and businesses fail.

Perhaps you've already learned this lesson the hard way or can sense that you're headed toward a crash. If the old ways of doing business are still working for you, know that they will not for much longer. Technology is ushering in a new age of collaboration, and with this, staying with the org chart is becoming a little riskier every day. The good news is that the answers are already here, and once you put them into practice, everything will change for the better. Your people will thrive and take your business along for the ride. You can harness the power of change.

ENTER THE BOT

In 2009, a new class of collaboration technologies quietly found their way into corporate life. Unfortunately, these innovative technologies were framed as little more than "Twitter, but for companies." Other people described them as chat platforms, likening them to text messages for businesses. Executives recoiled at these characterizations, seeing the platforms as a place for employees to waste time chatting, ignoring the massive amount of time we all waste in email. Security teams saw them as existential threats, despite the fact that they were demonstrably more secure than email.

This new collaboration model was revolutionary for human collaboration and teamwork. The ever-present complaint about the corrosive effects of silos at work vanishes with the proper rollout of something like Slack or Teams. Ephemeral teams form and dissolve in minutes to tackle problems without slow and expensive meetings. People collaborate more fluidly with one another without the need for management oversight.

What has been missed in all the talk about these collaboration platforms is that they enable bots to work with people as just another employee. Employees can reach out to bots operating in collaboration platforms whenever they need them, and those same bots can reach out to an employee the moment a bot is needed or needs something.

At this point you may have heard the term, but what exactly *is* a bot? According to Google, a bot is "an autonomous program on a network (especially the Internet) that can interact with computer systems or users, especially one designed to respond or behave like a player in an adventure game." One bot can tap into any number of powerful platforms to augment their human coworkers through collaboration platforms.

So why do bots, working in collaboration platforms, have such massive implications for the way businesses work and how they organize? Because bots can orchestrate exceedingly complex patterns of collaboration among humans at previously unachievable scales.

The primary responsibility of any manager, regardless of their position in the org chart, is orchestrating collaboration. A meeting is a technique for orchestrating collaboration. An email with a bunch of people in the "to" or "cc" line is yet another way to orchestrate collaboration. The scale to which this orchestration occurs today is a function of a manager's individual ability.

This individual ability plays a massive, unspoken role in how the org chart looks—too many direct reports can lead to sloppy operations, where "too many" is loosely defined as the *current* manager's ability to orchestrate collaboration within their team. Whenever you see a manager whose direct reports are also managers, one implication is that the complexity of orchestrating the collaboration of the individual contributors became too great, calling for another manager.

Bots, on the other hand, can orchestrate complex patterns of collaboration for ten to ten thousand people or more. Bots working at these scales can facilitate collaboration among large groups of people to solve any number of problems, including management functions like performance reviews, strategy execution, project management, etc.

CHAPTER ONE

UNEARTHING AN ADAPTIVE WORKPLACE

———

I became interested in the topic of new workplace organizational designs enabled by technology in 2004 when I was working as a business and strategy consultant at Perot Systems. Perot Systems was a world-class IT outsourcing company. Typically, when a business outsources their IT to another company, they hire away "key" managers and replace everyone else with employees from the outsourcing company to achieve economies of scale. Perot Systems did this too. For reasons it took me awhile to identify, I had the nagging feeling that there was something amiss with how we were servicing our clients. We talked to them about their businesses as though they were machines formed of processes, technologies, titles, and org charts.

What we did not discuss was the value built up over time in the relationships among the employees, like axons among neurons. I have no data to back this up, but I suspect that if you were to find a way to measure the amount of energy we all put into our working relationships, we might discover that this is where we are spending the majority of our energy every day. To torture the brain metaphor a bit more, there are roughly eighty-six times the number of axons in the brain than there are neurons.

Yet we never studied, leveraged, or even acknowledged the relationships and strong kinship that staff members had already established with one another. We completely overlooked the most essential element of any business—the relationship element and how the work was getting done. Each employee has value that is unlocked by their collaboration with others. The potential for each individual is embodied in their relationships. Productive relationships yield maximum potential. Unproductive relationships mute potential. Relationships are not peripheral to business results; they are *essential* to it. The hive is defined more by the way bees work with one another than by the individual bee.

Instead of thinking about any of this, Perot Systems did what most companies do—we treated employees like fungible cogs in a machine. The reasoning goes that if you have a manager over a department that produces widgets, and that person manages people who know how to produce widgets, then the most important asset is the manager who knows how to run a department of widget makers. After all, you can always find another widget maker. Replacing a widget maker should be seamless, right? Of course, it is anything but.

I realized that the org chart is almost incidental to how work actually gets done. Titles, promotions, and reporting lines all are components of an idealized machine for producing market value. Relationships are not in an org chart as a first-class entity the way a title is. Instead, they are implicit, assumed to be among members of a team. Yet these relationships govern how work gets done.

It was no surprise, then, that making decisions based exclusively on an org chart yielded suboptimal results. The more I saw our process result in bad staffing decisions, the more I realized something needed to change. I also suspected I knew exactly what we were missing. I thought back to a job I held in 1998, at a startup called the Technical Resource Connection (TRC), where I worked in a variety of roles, including information architect and technology consultant to C-suites. The organizational structure of TRC was flat, consisting of a general manager and a bunch of team members, each of whom held their own badge of honor within the company, which they'd genuinely earned. It was an extraordinarily egalitarian organization. Everyone was happy to pitch in however they could because we loved our tribe, and it felt good to contribute in both big and small ways to a cause we believed in, a cause bigger than ourselves.

Perot Systems ultimately bought TRC. As a consultant for Perot, I had the opportunity to study dozens of companies from a dozen different industries. The more I studied, the more I saw a recurring theme: Companies start out small, agile, and tribal. Collaboration is fast and effective. As the number of employees grows, the number of relationships increases exponentially and the collaboration model becomes unwieldy, and so they begin to use the only model they know how to scale—the org chart. With the org chart comes a transition from a tribal human organism to a machine formed from fungible components. The former can't scale while the latter can. At least it used to be that way before collaboration bots, but I'm getting ahead of myself.

THE POWER OF SOCIAL NETWORKS

In 2004, I had the opportunity to work with a fantastic CIO at a large, prestigious hospital system in Northern California. This hospital system intended to outsource its IT to Perot Systems. The CIO and I agreed that we were going to handle the staffing decisions differently because a seminal book—*The Hidden Power of Social Networks* by

Robert L. Cross and Andrew Parker—had just been published. The premise of the book is that work gets done through complex social networks that are fluid and have only a loose correlation to the org chart. It describes a methodology for mapping out how work actually gets done through what the authors called "social network analyses," commonly referred to today as organizational network analyses or ONAs. The book argues that a company benefits more by optimizing the fluidity of a network than by following the org chart.

To better understand how work got done, the CIO and I agreed we would try creating a social network analysis as spelled out in the book, ignoring titles and org charts. The results were shocking. We found that most of the work was getting done by people who had quietly developed a massive amount of influence, or soft power. The startup was still alive and kicking in plain sight if you knew where to look within this well-established hospital. It's just that, now, it was hidden inside the machine.

Below is an actual example of an organizational network analysis done using the first version of the Adaptive Engagement Platform.

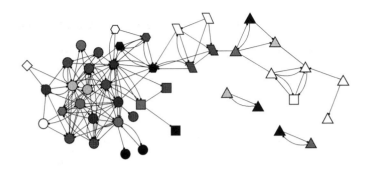

This diagram has no correlation to the org chart, but it does provide an incredibly accurate depiction of how work got done in these teams, of which there are several as indicated by the different shapes. Whereas I used to create these kinds of graphs manually, now chatbots collect and analyze all this data for me. There are lots of terrific books on network diagrams like the one above that I will touch on throughout this book. The focus of this book is how collaboration platforms and bots that operate inside of them are changing the way companies can organize themselves.

So, for now, the critical thing to consider is that the relationships depicted in the graph above outnumber the people; it is simple math—three people have potentially six relationships, and the number of potential relationships grows exponentially with each new person.

When you reorganize a team, you are potentially destroying a world of invisible value greater than what you can see, which is much more than the employees and their titles. Sometimes that might be a disaster (as would be the case with the circle team shown in the left half of the diagram), and sometimes that might be the right thing to do (in a case such as the triangle team). Incredibly, this kind of destruction happens every day without a second thought for the hidden value of the social networks.

This analysis led me to realize that reorganizing based only on org charts tears apart tribes that are getting work done, effectively lobotomizing the resulting organization and turning them into a zombie. Before acquisition or restructuring, tribes of people hang together, sometimes in terrible cultural environments, doing the best they can to deliver. By coming in and imposing new structures, processes, and organizational models, companies like Perot Systems inadvertently destroyed the very tribes that we needed to deliver value. In effect, we were laying waste the intelligence built up *in the existing tightly interwoven fabric of working relationships*. It's sad, really.

Mergers and acquisitions (M&A) often create this destruction of corporate value on an industrial scale. Outsourcing can inadvertently lobotomize one functional department of a company. M&A, on the other hand, have the potential to destroy everything in two companies. Raise your hand if you have survived a merger. Now keep your hand raised if the combined company was better than either one of the original companies. Really? Nobody? Well, of course not.

The worst mergers I've ever seen were the purest form of weaponizing the org chart. A team of outside consultants would come in and create a massive spreadsheet with the names of every employee, and columns for things like their titles, salaries, functional areas, and geographic location. To find redundancies, they sorted the spreadsheet by column and then deleted rows.

It was, in effect, a blender into which outside consultants unknowingly threw the company's most valuable and underrated asset—network knowledge. A prominent leader in the organization later said to me of this merger, "If you are running a dairy farm, stop killing the cows for their meat." This is a truly gruesome, but also apt, visual for what many companies do: they treat their employees like fungible farm animals.

This realization compelled me to study more deeply the fluidity of the social network within organizations and to devise ways to harness the collaboration I saw with technology. I needed to understand how we, as strategy consultants, could strengthen companies, rather than inadvertently lobotomizing them. At that time, the technologies I employed were clunky, hard to use, and a burden on the employees I studied. I was mostly relegated to spreadsheets for data collection and then used an ontology editor from the Stanford University informatics department called Protégé. These tools enabled me to do this on a small scale, but doing it at a large scale was a different problem entirely. I put the work to the side, but the idea kept nagging at me.

GOING GLOBAL

I left Perot Systems for new opportunities, but I continued to observe and collect data about social networks' fluidity. While the technologies continued to be burdensome, the social networks I studied always supplanted any org chart put in front of me. I knew those org charts didn't tell the story of how work *actually* gets done in a company, and that their rigidity ran counter to the fluidity necessary to compete effectively. I began operating my teams as simple social networks, optimizing the fluidity of the team based on its members' feedback. The results were impressive. The teams loved it. Their resiliency in the face of change was inspiring. I knew I was on to something.

In 2012, a friend of mine who is an amazing executive invited me to join his company to build an R&D team designed to change the company's position in the marketplace. He also challenged me to devise a way to improve the company's productivity ten times over. To put this challenge into context, most established companies are thrilled with single-digit percentage improvements. He was asking for something all but impossible—1,000 percent. What he proposed was nuts. He also told me that I could run the team in whatever way I saw fit.

There was just one caveat: I had to prove my model by applying it to a global team. This caveat was almost a deal breaker for me. To that point, I had not achieved satisfactory results from a global R&D team. Cultural and educational differences combined with distance and language barriers had always resulted in crippling issues. That largely remains true to this day using conventional techniques, but the siren song from potential opportunities in a global labor force is like executive catnip. Despite my reservations, I agreed and I am so glad I did. The Adaptive Experiment yielded amazing results from diverse, globally distributed teams.

By that point, I had worked with enough companies and seen enough processes to understand that process improvements would not be enough to accomplish my friend's lofty goal. I also knew there was not a clear technology play that, by itself, could achieve the necessary results. Both technology and process come into play when we're talking about productivity, but even combined, they are not enough to unlock the type of boon my colleague was looking for.

THE MECHANICAL BUSINESS PHILOSOPHY

There is one sector of business that can achieve the insane amount of productivity growth my friend was looking for: startups. Startups move fast because their collaboration models are simple—some might even say tribal. Decisions happen quickly, and the existential threat of being unemployed forces risk-taking. As companies grow, their collaboration models increase in complexity, and they resort to an org chart to machine the complexity. In the process, they lay waste to the tribal collaboration that helped them become successful in the first place.

So, how could we bring the best, most tribal elements of a startup into a company that had long since passed that stage of its evolution? I realized that part of the answer might be in crowdsourced organizational design. "What is crowdsourcing?" you ask? This is from Wikipedia: "*Crowdsourcing is a sourcing model in which individuals or organizations obtain goods and services, including ideas and finances, from a large, relatively open and often rapidly-evolving group of [users]; it divides work between participants to achieve a cumulative result.*"

Perhaps if I could create an environment in which employees could rapidly figure out how to achieve alignment themselves instead of looking to the hierarchy and bureaucracy to do so, we could get that startup magic at scale.

Crowdsourcing organizational design is how startups often operate. There is a rag-tag band of people, all of whom are passionate about some aspect of the company's value proposition. They are not focused on titles and hierarchy but are instead intent on achieving the common goal. In a startup, you are often simultaneously a follower and a leader. In other words, you are a servant to your colleagues, and they are servants to you. You are a leader for your colleagues, and they are leaders for you. You won't hear that it is "lonely at the top" in a startup, and, if you do, it likely won't be a successful startup.

When success comes and you need to scale, how do you do it? Today we tend to use the one and only technology we've relied on since it was invented by Scottish-American engineer Daniel McCallum in 1854—the org chart! Seriously, what else in business has survived for that amount of time? Everything else about how businesses operate has been creatively destroyed except the very idea of capitalism itself and the org chart!

Along with the org chart came a very distinct and unchallenged philosophy about businesses rooted in the time in which Daniel McCallum lived: businesses are machines that manufacture things. The workers are fungible cogs in the machine. Functional titles take priority over the parenthetical humans who hold those titles. There is no place for relationships in the org chart because the manager is orchestrating all collaboration to stamp out widgets. Despite everything that has changed in the last 165 years, we are still stuck in the org chart that casts all businesses as machines.

Not long after Daniel McCallum invented the org chart, Frederick Taylor, another influential figure, invented the Scientific Management philosophy. This philosophy is often referred to as Taylorism. Mr. Taylor is credited with bringing the scientific method to business, aggressively measuring every aspect of company throughput. If you ever want to see Taylorism in action and get a good laugh, watch Charlie Chaplin's *Modern Times* movie. I promise you will be simultaneously amused by Mr. Chaplin's comedic genius and horrified by how little things have changed.

Taylorism lasted a brief period of forty years or so, but his work continues to resonate in more contemporary methodologies like Six Sigma and Total Quality Management (TQM). So, while Daniel McCallum gave us a way to model the components of the mechanical business, Frederick Taylor gave us a way to optimize the mechanical business. This combination is something I refer to as the mechanical business philosophy that has dominated organizational design for more than a century.

The mechanical business philosophy treats businesses

like machines and the people inside them as machine parts. This dehumanizing perspective has led to amazing manufacturing advancements and stunning examples of bad corporate behavior. More on this later.

Despite increasingly obvious flaws, the mechanical business philosophy was an advancement over what preceded it for manufacturing. Ironically, it is now bringing about its own demise. It was the mechanical business philosophy that drove manufacturing marvels like the computer, the internet, and now elastic platforms like Amazon Web Services (AWS). Combined, those technologies are ushering in a new age when that which can be treated like a machine part will instead be automated.

To expand on this, we are entering an era when robots and bots will make us human again by freeing us from repetitive, rote tasks that require robotic precision. Bots can help us collaborate in complex new ways at scale, enabling companies to solve much bigger problems. In this new era, bots will drive much higher demand for individual human creativity, which in turn will usher in demand for large-scale, bot-orchestrated creativity among many people.

Despite its dehumanizing effect, the mechanical business philosophy served humanity well during the Industrial Revolution but began losing its luster at the dawn of the Information Age. Yet we've clung to its gleaming promise of mechanical execution and robotic discipline from humans.

Let's take a simple allegory of the family road trip. Before 2005, you mapped out your trip and then assigned someone with the robotic task of watching the map and giving directions. Those of you who lived in these dark times can remember the angst this dynamic caused. On a trip from Florida to Mississippi to visit my parents, I awoke from a nap to ask my wife where we were, and she responded, "We are making great time! We are already to Georgia!" For the map-savvy among you, we should have never been in Georgia on our way to Mississippi from Florida. Then, in 2005, Google Maps came out, and we all outsourced this robotic task to a robot. Now, augmented by a bot, we can all simply enjoy the trip without the anxiety. We now have the luxury of being bored.

Offloading rote, robotic tasks to machines will de-emphasize the need for humans to stand in as robots and lead to a greater emphasis on applying new forms of skill acquisition and performance improvements. With the emergence of these innovative technologies, we are at the end of the mechanical business philosophy era and have entered a new era of organic business philosophy, a philosophy I call Adaptive.

Adaptive views business as a technology-enabled organism. Instead of looking at a business as a mechanic might look at a car, we look at a business like a holistic doctor might look at a patient. Instead of looking at a business as a collection of cogs in a machine, we look at a business as an organism that is living, breathing, emotional, and formed from a rich web of human relationships. Those humans are augmented by bots and robots, which free humans from work requiring mechanical discipline and enable them to focus on collaborating with one another to solve bigger problems.

This new Adaptive philosophy is ushering in a new world of organizational designs, the likes of which I can only begin to imagine. *The first iteration of a new organizational design is that of self-organizing teams augmented by bots that orchestrate complex patterns of collaboration to solve increasingly bigger problems.* The rest of this book will explore the massive, tectonic shift implied by that last sentence.

We are already seeing the edges of Adaptive emerging, but until now we didn't know what to call it. We also haven't known quite what to do about it. Instead, we have spent inordinate amounts of money on improving engagement scores yet have continued to have wildly disengaged employees. We have finally begun reconciling the horrid behavior enabled by those granted the positional power to treat their subordinates like machine parts. Even that word, "subordinate," is dehumanizing. In short, businesses are being driven to acknowledge, accommodate, and harness the humanity that has been hiding in the machine all along.

ENTER ADAPTIVE

With all of this in mind, my goal was to find a way to create healthy *business organisms* that can rapidly evolve and compete by solving increasingly bigger problems. Such an environment would require employees to collaborate in new complex ways, lift each other up, benefit from support provided by teams of servant leaders, and harness the motivation and sense of ownership and bonding that come from how startups organize their work. It is these elements that underlie the tribal nature of startups and their ability to move fast and get things done. At the very heart of all effective collaboration is something simple—empathy and trust.

Empathy, or the ability to understand and share the feelings of another, and trust are irrelevant in the mechanical business because there is simply no natural place for them. You won't find either in the org chart, but that is the most prominent feature in a social network diagram.

In an org chart, you are to do what the manager says, and

in return, the manager, and only the manager, decides your reward (such as a raise or promotion) or your punishment (such as a demotion or termination). There is no room for trust. Empathy is not needed and, in fact, can run counter to what it takes to get ahead in corporate life. The importance of empathy and trust are an afterthought, bolted on afterward in the form of things like sensitivity training and after the point when everyone realizes how critical these commodities are to success. They're not built into the system, just clumsily attached.

For two years, Google studied what it takes to make awesome teams that can go fast. They found that psychological safety—empathy and trust—lies at the heart of teams like this. Empathy creates servant leaders, tremendous colleagues, and breakout team performance. Trust allows people to speak their mind without fear of retribution and then move fast, fast, fast. So, the question becomes, *how do you scale empathy and trust?* If you guessed bots, you guessed right, but I didn't realize that right away.

That brings us back to my friend's business and my decision to take on his challenge to increase productivity by 1,000 percent and help them find a new market position. At the time I joined my friend's company, the Big Data movement was an emerging phenomenon. I decided it was time to recast our company as a data-analytics company and build the company's very first analytics team. I constructed the team in such a way that every person was positioned as a servant leader accountable for helping their colleagues achieve greatness. This model also ensured that we were all accountable to one another to level up and deliver. Typical management and human resources functions were crowdsourced on a peer-to-peer level. Team members contributed to one another's day-to-day productivity and long-term growth. They kept each other accountable. With this, the team enjoyed that old tribal collaboration magic, even within the confines of a larger company that was entrenched in a hierarchy and all the things that come with it.

This adaptive structure allowed us to move quickly and nimbly, adjust to changes in the market and technology, and act decisively to utilize the resources at our disposal. We were enthusiastic and had a sense of ownership because we could put our knowledge and expertise to use rather than being told what to do—regardless of whether those instructions were the best way forward and best use of team skills. Now we were flying an F-16. In fact, we even named this big data initiative F-16.

For the first time in ten years, the company experienced its first massive market change as this new team brought the big data wave crashing to our shores. The team I built, using what turned out to be the initial Adaptive model, lit the fuse to a massive rocket we had strapped to the company, and...everyone freaked out. The rest of the company was completely unprepared for what happened next.

That early data analytics bent the arc of the company's destiny, and the entire business sold for several billion dollars a few years later. It went public after merging with another company. We tried to replicate the big data magic with a deeply hierarchical organization, but that failed to deliver. Regardless, the company was bought again for several more billions and finally taken private again. All told, these transactions yielded a seven-times return. Not bad for a project started with a team of ten people.

The company continued to fly at breakneck speeds. I rolled out the model for other teams. The teams using the Adaptive model were fluid, quickly crowdsourcing new organizational designs to accommodate the seemingly monthly changes in technology and market trends. The rest of the company still operated within a well-established org chart and was vehemently resistant to change and, unsurprisingly, resulted in little material progress.

In fact, the Adaptive teams began to rapidly evolve away from the org chart team. I saw this happen enough times that I later referred to it as the "Adaptive Redshift Effect," a reference to the shift in reflected light caused by celestial bodies rapidly moving away from the observer. The Adaptive Redshift Effect became such a pronounced phenomenon, I began to note it as a dynamic that required early, proactive mitigation, which I'll cover later in chapter 8, "Common Hurdles."

During these chaotic times, the company commissioned an engagement survey. Studies have shown that companies with high levels of employee engagement yield better financial results than companies with low engagement. This was my first real, independent measure of the Adaptive Experiment's effectiveness.

The results were jaw-dropping. The team using the Adaptive model enjoyed an engagement score in the high eighties. The rest of the company lingered at sixty—the industry average—and some parts of the company were in the forties. Engagement fluctuated for the rest of the company, but it remained stable for teams using the Adaptive model throughout all the turmoil wrought by the acquisitions.

The company hired a change-management consultant who studied the Adaptive model. She had previously worked with NASA on their change initiatives. Her report stated that she'd never seen a more passionate, engaged group of workers in her life. What she saw was empathy and trust at scale, made possible in part by bots operating in the collaboration platform we adopted.

Outside of these measurable results, I saw the entire team come alive with passion. We loved working with one another and being part of a fast-moving tribe. People who came to work with us from the hierarchy relished the opportunity to operate in the Adaptive model with its quirky collection of bots. All this happened despite massive, near-monthly changes and a revolving door of executives.

People who were part of the original six-year Adaptive Experiment went on to secure prominent positions with other companies, specifically because of the servant-leadership experience they got from Adaptive. Other participants told me that they grew more in nine months inside of Adaptive than they had in the preceding three years with the company.

Candidates we turned away came back later to ask for a copy of the Adaptive handbook so they could emulate it at their new company. Countless candidates have told us they will happily take less money for the opportunity to work for our company because it sounded like nirvana!

The first year of the experiment, I ran this model manually, slowly gathering requirements for the bots I knew I would need to build. It was labor intensive but manageable for a small team. As the dramatic results of the experiment came into focus, I realized that I needed bots to help me scale up the complex collaboration patterns that had begun to emerge. That was when I decided to build the prototype for the Adaptive Engagement Platform.

FROM MECHANIC TO DOCTOR

Many books about employee engagement and organization are academic, written by someone outside of the corporate world who is observing and theorizing about the day-to-day mechanisms of business and workplace culture or who has observed models that appear to work.

This book is not that. I had the rare opportunity to run the Adaptive Experiment for six years, which yielded the model around which I later built the Adaptive Engagement Platform. We started by using what I had learned from the preceding year and from similar models at Valve and Pixar. We rapidly iterated through hundreds of changes in response to an equal number of experiments. When we saw improvements, we would describe a hypothesis, set up an experiment, and prove or disprove the hypothesis. We always treated Adaptive like an experiment.

The information you'll find here is based on fifteen years of in-the-trenches research and six years of intense applied research and development. All these strategies have been applied in corporations and in partnership with HR professionals. And not just any corporations, but highly regulated corporations that are more conservative and entrenched in traditional hierarchical behavior than most.

The Adaptive model that served as the foundation of the Adaptive Engagement Platform consistently raised engagement scores within those organizations from the forty to sixty range to the high eighties and produced breakout results.

As you read this book and consider rolling out some of the principles from the Adaptive model in your own company, keep in mind that this is not a one-and-done process. At the heart of this is cultivating human beings and their relationships with one another. You must monitor the health of your teams and their relationships. You must ensure that your business thrives but also that the human beings who make it run *and* their relationships with one another thrive as well. Too many companies today fail to recognize a fact that is right in front of their faces: businesses are organisms composed of individuals with gifts, passions, anxieties, challenges, and, most importantly, relationships. When we holistically address these things on an ongoing basis, the results are profound. A new class of technologies enables us to do this very thing, whereas before it would have been exceedingly difficult and unsustainable.

Does this require more of you than it would to promote a selection of employees to managerial positions and let them run the show? Yes and no. Instead of being a mechanic, you must be a doctor who is able to see and understand the web of relationships as a first-class entity, courtesy of your friendly neighborhood bots. Just as you see potential and value in an individual employee, you should see even more potential and value in their relationships. In other words, given two people, you have three things to cultivate holistically—the two people and their relationship with each other. Managing all these things individually is simply too much for any organization to handle—without bots.

While the systems you'll read about in this book require you to remain consistently on top of cultivating team members and relationships, there is also an element of self-regulation and accountability built into all of this, also facilitated by bots. This makes the systems simultaneously easier and more difficult than those you are using right now. Administrative burdens will shrink dramatically in some ways, while your focus on people and relationships will increase proportionally.

One of the things I've learned while operating in the Adaptive model is that administering an org chart is easier than coaching employees. The former is a rote task that most managers can do in their sleep (a perfect target for a bot). The latter requires creativity, focus, discipline, and mindfulness (a perfect target for a human). So, if you can offload the repetitive stuff to a bot, then the hours in your day don't change, but the work you do is more mentally challenging.

CHAPTER TWO

THE BIRTH OF HIERARCHY

———

We have already begun to explore the faults of the mechanical business philosophy and will continue to do so in the coming pages. An important part of transformation is understanding *how* the status quo is fundamentally broken so that we can do a more effective job of fixing it.

Before we go any further, I want to be clear that we all owe a deep debt of gratitude to both Daniel McCallum and Frederick Taylor as well as everyone who inspired and refined their work. These individuals helped usher in an era of manufacturing that has changed the world. I'm quite sure both of these men were informed by other influential characters of their time, and we owe them our thanks, too, even if they have been lost in the mists of time.

So, with deep gratitude to the mechanical business philosophy, let's explore how it is failing us in this emerging new era of Adaptive.

We don't tolerate dysfunction in other areas of life the way we do at work. I would go so far as to say we even *expect* dysfunction at work. Not only that, but we joke about it with a variety of gallows humor unique to the workplace. We must, otherwise we'd all go insane.

For nearly thirty years, the comic strip *Dilbert* has been satirizing workplace culture. Over time, *Dilbert* has branched out into a television series, books, a video game, and mountains of merchandise. *Dilbert*'s success has hinged on its relatability and gallows humor about the workplace. Although *Dilbert* is among the most recognizable, there are plenty of other examples of workplace jabs in pop culture. They usually include an idiot boss, a feckless coworker, and bad behavior that is endlessly tolerated because...?

Cynical workplace humor is also embedded in our language in ways that are so common that most of us probably don't even think about what we're saying anymore. You've heard all of the jargon: Monday Morning Blues, Hump Day Wednesday, Faux Friday (Thursday's excuse to drink), and, of course, TGIF. There is even a restaurant named after that last one. Apparently, the only day that doesn't deserve a misery-ladened moniker is Tuesday. So, enjoy Tuesday, everyone!

Why is work universally recognized as such a miserable experience?

I would argue that it comes down to the dehumanizing effect of the mechanical business philosophy that expects robotic performance from organic humans. Most businesses today are set up as hierarchical organizations. In a hierarchy of any variety, positional power is bestowed by someone from up "above." Some people earn this power by coming up through the ranks of a company, but that is rarely the case. Many companies hire executives and managers from outside, conferring positional power upon someone outside the tribe. Understandably, this is met with great consternation from those people within who have already established a proven record of dedicating their time and energy to the organization. These are the people who intimately understand the business and nuances of how it functions. And, yet, a stranger from outside of the company is appointed to lead.

Bringing in outsiders to lead in a workplace sets up a weird dysfunction. It flies in the face of how humans have operated for the past one hundred thousand years. Historically, great leaders earn the right to lead, but the hierarchical concept goes against self-determination, an inalienable right over which wars have been fought and the US Declaration of Independence was written. Yet, in work situations, the message is that if we step outside the boundaries of established hierarchy, we will be in trouble (literally), an experience more commonly found in authoritarian regimes.

Let us take a typical workplace situation where this all plays out. I once witnessed a misguided executive who was brought in from the outside to bark at his team, "The CEO appointed me to lead this group, and until he removes me, that is exactly what I intend to do!" The executive was reacting to direct reports who believed there were less-expensive and easier paths to achieving a goal put forth by the board. Unable to *persuade* his direct reports with the power of his idea, the executive instead deployed his positional power. Sir, yes sir.

That executive ended up costing the company close to $100 million and wreaking immeasurable damage. The executive team summarily fired the executive, which, in a sense, further disengaged employees. Had the executive team only listened to their screams into the darkness, they could have avoided the damage. Situations like this eradicate any semblance of trust and empathy within the team and result in uninformed decisions that cost companies many millions of dollars. Worst of all, everyone was miserable, and the brain-drain was something to behold.

THE TROUBLE WITH POWER

A famous quote from the book *Animal Farm* reads, "Power corrupts. Absolute power corrupts absolutely." This is certainly the case in many workplaces today because their structure inherently promotes power mongering or "protecting turf." Because of these power dynamics, hierarchical organizations draw out all sorts of terrible behaviors. This can manifest in significant issues like sexual harassment and hostile work environments. This behavior would never fly in a different type of organizational structure where a system of checks and balances exists to foster empathy and trust. If someone in the tribe violates empathy and trust, others will check them.

A perfect example of corruption by power is clear in the #metoo movement that began in 2017 and led to a tsunami of stories about truly abhorrent behavior by people in positions of appointed power. I applaud the individuals who had the bravery to begin tearing down these corrosive power structures. I also know that the #metoo movement was only the tip of an enormous iceberg. A colleague of mine was in line for a promotion. She has thirty years of experience in her industry, her team has the highest engagement scores in her company, and she is a demonstrated servant leader. She also repeatedly rejected the sexual advances of her chief operating officer, who scuttled her promotion in retribution. She never reported him. When I asked why, her answer was simple:

as a single parent and the sole breadwinner for her family, she couldn't risk standing up to a powerful executive. I wonder how women have silently endured the atrocious behavior of those with power over their job security, their pay raises, and for mothers their children's futures.

My colleague wasn't the only one who was being harassed, however, and the executive was later fired. Another woman in a less-vulnerable position held the COO accountable. Neither of these women realized that the other was mired in the same personal and professional drama. Had I not known her, only 50 percent of the story might ever be known—another woman mysteriously unable to climb the corporate ranks.

Firing these cretins and implementing sensitivity training with teeth will treat the symptoms. Abandoning positional power in favor of a new model that can scale empathy and trust bolstered by dispassionate bots targets the disease itself.

Power corrupts and erodes effectiveness in more mundane ways, too, such as when a new executive brought into a company wreaks havoc by weaponizing their newly appointed position of power during their initial "storming phase." When this happens, business flounders and a new person is appointed in their place. Even if this new executive is wonderful, a whipsaw effect occurs. The company's culture is always changing because that culture is dictated by the person in power.

What confounds me completely is that those of us in democratic countries regularly rail against regimes governed by personality cults—North Korea, Nazi Germany, Fascist Italy, Stalinist Russia. Yet, when it comes to business, we expect—and in fact cheer—personality cults. Steve Jobs, Elon Musk, and Larry Ellison are all examples of CEOs who rule with an iron fist. Instead of mass, we instead have summary firings. A CEO can destroy stock prices with a single tweet. Yet we continue to see personality-cult companies as a "good thing." Meanwhile, these personalities are destroying "legacy value," or the durable part of a business that investors want to buy. It is what sticks around, even as managers and leaders come and go.

Too often, people who are key to the success of the hierarchical organization leave because they are discouraged and feel devalued. When they leave, it creates a negative fall-out effect for every person beneath them in the hierarchy, which damages legacy value. It is also detrimental to business results. We've all seen this happen—a key player in a company leaves, and both morale and business suffer as a result. Everything changes.

Yet hierarchies not only allow this to happen, but they also *breed* it. It's so strange when you think about it: businesses are generally risk-averse to everything, yet they are willing to place all of their bets on a handful of power figures in a hierarchy. The legacy value of a company is just one bad executive away from being destroyed.

It does not have to be like this.

Hierarchies operate as simple "rules of the road" that anyone can follow. The rise of bots that can operate in collaboration platforms opens up new, more complex and fluid organizational models that can self-adjust based on simple heuristics of sophisticated machine-learning algorithms. A hierarchy only changes when a handful of humans change it in a way that they *think* will yield better results. In a bot-augmented fluid organization, the value and knowledge are cultivated from the social network as a whole (relationships and all), rather than from a single individual. In this way, bots can inform the individuals so that they can make the best local decisions without an org chart or managerial oversight.

The result is a resilient network that can crowdsource the solution to complex problems. Individuals strengthen the social network while they are there, and that value remains after they leave. Networks are resilient and fluid, while hierarchies are brittle and rigid. Legacy value is in the hands of the many, not a select few, any one of whom could use their positional power to lay waste to everything below them. Because soft power is earned, it can easily be given *and* taken away (this is key). As a result, individuals are less likely to abuse soft power than positional power.

.

Another issue with hierarchies is that they place employees in a position where their future success is in the hands of one person who is "in charge" of them, their manager. The issues here are many and obvious, but let's look at just one example of how this can play out. I have a friend we will call Ellie, who manages fifty people at her company—more people than anyone else in the organization. Ellie does an excellent job with this and has for a long time. Still, she is consistently passed over for a vice-presidential position. Ellie's previous manager told her he would advocate for her promotion, but he then left the company and was replaced by a stranger with a completely different opinion about what it takes to be a vice president. Now Ellie is stuck, completely reliant on her new manager to lift her up to the next level. Unfortunately, he has not done so, for reasons that are unclear. Since they are unclear, Ellie cannot do anything to address them and remains stuck, day in and day out, feeling as if her future is completely out of her control. She reminds me of Alice from Dilbert—an imminently qualified employee who is trying to speak sanity to an insane system.

Ellie's situation is not unique. Hierarchical companies

often skip over the most deserving employees for promotions. This can occur for any number of reasons. Their boss just does not like them, even though their colleagues do. That person's promotion would make them more marketable to competitors, and their boss wants to keep them in a specific position at the company. Sometimes what I call "key person syndrome" occurs where an employee is great at what they do, and they also happen to be the only person who knows how to do that job. They become stuck precisely *because* of how good they are; the company cannot risk moving them to another position without a negative impact. It is the career equivalent of a Chinese Finger Trap.

In an ideal world, everyone would be singularly focused on shared common goals that drive the company strategy, and we would reward people for securing and deploying new skills that help drive that strategy. People want recognition for their contributions. They want to feel that their work, time, and energy make an impact. If companies could adopt a title system that precisely described the contributions each employee made to a company, through both their unique skillset and their personality, I think everyone would be much happier.

This isn't how it works in corporate life today. Instead, companies hire people for a title. They often bring a bucket of other qualities and skills they could bring to the company, but those things are ignored and sometimes even discouraged. "Stay in your lane!" you may be told, either implicitly or explicitly. The employee then feels discounted as a human being and begins to disengage. Who wouldn't?

Hierarchies breed the desire to climb the ladder. Again, it goes back to that human desire for self-determination. The higher our title, the more power we have over others and the less power *other* people have over our destiny. I often wonder which is more important—more power over others or less power by others over you? In many ways, work can be likened to a form of hazing—survive working in the trenches for long enough, and one day you will get that cushy management position.

In hierarchies, the unit of recognition is the title, and the title is tied to salary. If an employee feels their value is not aligned with their title, they are likely to become disengaged. This works both ways: when employees see a boss with a high title contributing less to the company than they do, they also disengage. Meanwhile, how is any of this leading to more effective and efficient strategy execution?

WHERE MECHANICAL BUSINESSES WIN

In some ways, mechanical businesses can be very efficient. If the CEO is exactly right about how to capture a market, and every single manager knows exactly how to make that happen, a mechanical business can move with blinding speed. Everyone just asks, "How high?" when told to jump.

Unfortunately, the number of times this has happened could be counted on fingers and maybe a few toes. Yet optimism leads us to believe that *our business is that unicorn and we are the gods that will make it happen.*

Also, human beings do not like stasis. In the movie *Joe Versus the Volcano*, the protagonist Joe works in a horrible factory filled with abrasive blinking lights. He is stuck in that factory, stuck in his career, until an existential risk to his life jars him awake. Many of us have found ourselves in that situation at one point or another in our lives. We are not advancing or learning anything new, and we don't have a sense of self-determination. We're just treading water. We are Joe.

In the business world, promotions tap into this human desire for forward movement. Mechanical businesses provide a hierarchical structure within which people can level up. Whether they do so by upgrading their position in a single company or hopping from one company to the next, leveling up is the objective. This is important because you need a workforce that is constantly working to improve itself and then sticking around to exploit those improvements. Otherwise you will always be relegated to hiring new skills from the outside, a very risky prospect indeed.

The military does a respectable job at this. Military personnel know exactly what they need to do to advance their careers and increase their rank. Consequently, most of the military personnel I know are always working on some certification, taking a class, or deploying to a certain location to get the experience they need for their next promotion.

In fact, we can credit the Roman Empire with inventing the military hierarchy, which surely inspired Daniel McCallum when he invented the corporate org chart around the time of the American Civil War. The Romans needed to control vast expanses of territory from Rome and then, later, Constantinople. A key to their success was the military hierarchy. However, the military's mission is far narrower than that of the average corporation.

Mechanical businesses are particularly good at control. The org chart itself is a passive control mechanism. "Whom do you report to?" is quite a common question in corporate life. It acknowledges that you are a subordinate, controlled by an org-chart enforcer, also known as the manager. In the absence of the means for employees to manage themselves, say by augmenting them with bots, this kind of centralized control was essential to efficient operations.

Hierarchies also serve as a crude communication plan. When the CEO wants to see a change, the change is communicated down through the hierarchy. Each manager communicates the change to their direct reports, who tries to implement the directive in their own way. This can be efficient and, in the absence of other communication mediums, serves a critical role.

Finally, mechanical businesses are also exceptionally good at paperwork. While this may sound tongue-in-cheek, the truth is that most companies with more than three employees generate a lot of paperwork. This includes a wide range of matters, from compliance to training to reviews. All the processes that involve paperwork are necessary for the continuation and growth of a company. This said, you know what is even better at paperwork than humans? Bots.

EVOLVING BEYOND THE HIERARCHY

So here we are, well into the twenty-first century and one hundred years away from the arrival of the first faster-than-light starship as anticipated by *Star Trek: Enterprise*, trying to manage our businesses with technologies developed more than 150 years ago.

In a hierarchy, not only is emotional intelligence, or emotional quotient (EQ), unimportant, but the system often rewards people with a *low* EQ. Egotistical and narcissistic personalities are often rewarded because they are willing to exert the brute force required to get things done. This, regardless of discordance and despite the damage to relationships, is the most valuable asset of every company. This makes sense when you think about it. If you are trying to get robotic performance from your workforce to manufacture goods, and you don't have robots because it is 1854, then emotional intelligence is at the bottom of your list of things to worry about.

But it isn't 1854 anymore. Robots increasingly do manufacturing. Knowledge workers are more prevalent than assembly-line workers. Bots are everywhere now. As I write this, a bot pops in occasionally to give me spelling and grammar advice. Despite these tectonic shifts, think about how many infamous CEOs have risen to power who fit the low-EQ mold. Stories about screaming tantrums, humiliated employees, and other chest-beating behaviors are common folklore. Yet corporate culture applauds these "titans of industry" for their machismo. When you are trying to get unnatural robotic execution from humans, this kind of behavior is one way to get it.

I often wonder if this bias against emotional intelligence and empathy contributes to the scarcity of women in positions of corporate power. Between 2011 and 2015, Korn Ferry, a large management consulting firm headquartered in Los Angeles, performed a study that found that women scored higher than men on nearly all emotional intelligence competencies, with the exception of self-control, where no gender differences were observed.

Think about this conundrum: women outperform men on emotional intelligence. Emotional intelligence is a key ingredient of psychological safety. Psychological safety is a key ingredient of creating rich tapestries of relationships foundational to high-performing teams. Yet hierarchies devalue emotional intelligence. Had we developed organizational structures that capitalized on emotional intelligence and exploited the natural talents of women, we might all have summer homes on Mars by now.

A lot has happened since the dawn of the Information Age. In just the past few decades, we have seen fundamental shifts in the labor market, technology, and the type of work that most companies perform. Technology and automation handle most of the manufacturing and production work these days, and this will only accelerate with the emergence of increasingly powerful machine-learning algorithms. The implication is that companies are racing to offload repetitive, rote work to bots and robots, which is giving us time to pursue more creative work. Software development, marketing, and advertising all fall under this umbrella of today's creative Information Age economy.

Many companies no longer manage the creation of physical assets; instead, they are managing the creation of intellectual property. It's not an assembly line that needs to be managed but a creative process to be fostered. This takes companies away from the need to focus on an individual's assembly-line production output and, instead, requires them to facilitate and nurture a collaborative experience. And *this* requires a new emphasis on emotional intelligence in the business world to collaborate more effectively.

Another thing to consider: primary-school education recognizes this trend and is educating future workers in new ways. They're not just learning rote functions like reading, writing, and arithmetic. They're being taught concepts such as how to share their feelings with the world in a healthy, productive way. When she was about seven years old, my daughter told me her school was teaching her about "I-Messages." The idea being that when someone hurts you emotionally, you should help the offending party understand the impact of their actions in the form of a subjective statement—"I am upset because you did..." When I was her age, I learned to handle such situations with a schoolyard fight.

The result is new workers educated on building productive relationships. Consequently, younger generations enter the workforce with a separate set of expectations than earlier generations did. They want—and even expect—a workplace that resonates with the type of values they've been taught. Values like collaboration and EQ are important to them, as is the concept of legacy value. They want a leader who will nurture them, as opposed to just telling them what to do. They want to leave an indelible mark, not just serve as another cog in the mechanical business machine. The Adaptive workforce is already here.

SOMETHING ISN'T RIGHT

You've probably already felt the shift I'm talking about in your own work life, even if you've never put words to it. For many of us, we feel that something isn't working for us as individuals. We experience a general feeling of unhappiness surrounding work. We feel disconnected, disengaged, and sapped of energy or motivation. Some of us even feel angry and dehumanized. Some of us are driven to inhuman acts, and I often wonder if it is a reaction to being dehumanized by work.

This is a people problem, but it's also a business problem. It doesn't take much work to find horror stories about poorly performing businesses with egotistical managers and executives that make money despite their atrocious behavior. Repeatedly, studies have found a strong correlation between high engagement scores and great business outcomes. If your employees aren't engaged, the ramifications are likely clear in your company's productivity and bottom line.

My research has repeatedly proven that employee disengagement is often a measure of their unhappiness with the org chart and the impact that chart has on life inside the mechanical business. This discontent presents itself in many ways, but one of the most common ways I can find is through how people answer this single question: *How do you get promoted in this company?* I often hear answers like, "Well, you quit, go to another company, and then come back."

This is a huge red flag. It's difficult for employees to feel engaged with or dedicated to a company that they know won't recognize them for their advancements. This is a clear violation of empathy and trust. If they want more pay or responsibility, it involves making a leap to another company.

Another clear sign that things aren't working is the ever-increasing exodus of employees from corporate America in favor of the gig economy. The gig economy is a labor market characterized by the prevalence of short-term contracts or freelance work, orchestrated by software platforms and bots. Of course, technology plays a role in the gig economy as well, but if people were engaged with their work and their company, I think they would remain for the stability and fellowship. Think about it for a minute: in droves, people are choosing uncertainty over corporate stability. *That* is how valuable self-determination is. It's also a testament to how broken the current business model is.

CHANGE IS ON THE HORIZON

The problem is that most people don't have an answer to these two questions: how else could we organize, and how do we do it? If businesses don't follow the traditional hierarchical organizational structure, then what *do* they organize themselves around? For most companies, deviating from how businesses and other organizations have been structuring themselves for more than a century feels like a risky prospect. What they do not consider, however, is that operating a mechanical business in the Information Age and the new gig economy is even riskier.

For most companies and leadership teams, none of this is news. They are already well aware that something isn't working. They see it in their business results, turnover, and lack of engagement. They don't see a clear alternative other than repeatedly restructuring their company every time there is some dramatic new shift, such as a merger or a new technology that disrupts their business. But here's the thing—dramatic new shifts are coming at us almost every quarter now. Powerful platforms like AWS, Azure, and Google Compute Engine (GCE) enable small startups to destroy entire industries on a shoestring budget. Every technology component necessary to destroy any information-based business can be found in these platforms. Globalization means these startups can be based anywhere in the world, affording billions of people the opportunity to lay waste to your business. These changes are coming at us every day, but we can't respond by reorganizing our mechanical businesses every day. Mechanical businesses cannot do this, but Adaptive businesses can.

We find ourselves at a remarkably interesting moment in time. Boomers are exiting the workforce. The young and up-and-coming workforce has a markedly separate set of values than the workforce of twenty years ago. This new workforce is trained to operate in teams. They're all about EQ. And what EQ translates into is soft power to build powerful networks of relationships—not the authoritarian sort of power that hierarchical organizations use to drive robotic behavior from humans.

Many have not yet realized how powerful Information Economy tools really are. Collaboration platforms like Slack and Microsoft Teams can revolutionize organizations and replace some of the necessary elements that the hierarchy currently provides, such as management and administration. This isn't to say that leaders and bosses won't exist anymore. They will, but with their mechanical functions taken care of by technology, they'll have the time and bandwidth to put their efforts into being coaches. They will have the latitude to engage with team members and help them grow.

I'm already seeing this transformation happen at scale. Stand over the shoulder of someone using Slack in any company, and you will see it happening right before your eyes. Ephemeral, multidisciplinary teams are quickly forming to address problems and challenges as they arise and then are dissolving. CEOs are chatting directly with employees at scale versus down through the org chart. People are working with bots as though they were just another coworker.

The question for you is, do you want this to wash over your company, or do you want to harness this power proactively for a distinct competitive advantage? I believe it is these technologies that have brought the corporate world to a tipping point, where the model we'll discuss throughout the rest of this book is a potential reality for most businesses.

We can't ignore the very practical realities of what it

means to run a business, whether mechanical, Adaptive, or otherwise. Regulated industries must perform compliance activities. Human resources and legal concerns must be accounted for. And, of course, businesses need to turn a profit.

There *is* a way to have it all. There is a way to create a work environment that resonates with the up-and-coming workforce, leverages the powerful changes in collaboration technologies and the bots that can operate inside them, and allows companies to successfully harness the power of empathy and trust at scale. Now, it's just up to today's business leaders to catch up with what is available.

It's also important to note that while these questions of how to effectively organize in a new world are prescient for businesses today, I also think the world is trying to figure out how to organize and adapt to all the changes of the past couple of decades. How do we best use all the new technology at our disposal? In what ways have these technologies intrinsically changed our lives, how we relate, and how we work?

On some level, we are all trying to figure out how to better organize our personal lives, our social lives, and even our political structure. This can seem overwhelming because it requires an entirely new way of doing things and that we move much faster. These are big questions we can't ignore. The world is moving forward at a breakneck speed, and there is zero chance it will slow down without some cataclysmic event, at which point company profits will be the least of our concerns.

In this book, we will discuss how we can organize our working lives in such a way that everyone wins. Employees will be more fulfilled, business leaders will be able to do a more effective job and feel greater levels of satisfaction and gratification, and business results will improve in measurable ways.

CHAPTER THREE

ENTER TECHNOLOGY

———

The transition away from the mechanical business philosophy is *already underway*. It just isn't being harnessed effectively because we didn't understand the implications when it arrived. To see this change for yourself, go stand over the shoulder of someone using Slack, Teams, or any of the other "collaboration through messaging" technologies blazing into the workplace. You will see the future of work unfolding before your eyes:

- People solving big problems one micro-thin slice at a time
- Ephemeral teams forming and collapsing within hours or days
- People sharing interesting articles with each other to help everyone level up
- People goofing off in channels dedicated to fun (the new water cooler)

- People collaborating with smart chatbots as though they were coworkers

This kind of collaboration has quickly become the primary tool to move quickly and stay competitive. Demand for this form of collaboration is so strong, I'll bet that it is already operating on some scale in your company (whether you know it or not).

I first encountered this form of communication in 2012 with a product that has since been swallowed up by a larger competitor. That was when I knew I could use it to scale empathy and trust to create high-performance Adaptive teams. It was the one missing piece for me. It enabled me to augment every employee, no matter how many, with bots that helped them work in more fluid ways. These bots enabled me to harness what was already happening.

But it isn't just these new collaboration technologies that are changing how work gets done in a big, big way. Workforce demographics are changing at a breathtaking pace, accelerated by a whole bevy of automation technologies. In 1938 Congress passed the Fair Labor Standards Act that outlawed child labor, which had been prevalent to that point because automation was so limited, leading to high labor demands. In 1950, 30 percent of all jobs were manufacturing jobs that someone with a high-school diploma could perform. In 1950 only 7 percent of men and 5 percent of women had a college degree. Because workers tended to be young, most didn't have a particularly sophisticated worldview. They were expected to come to work, perform rote behaviors like putting something on a conveyor belt or taking something off a loading dock, and go home. For the average person, work didn't require much thought. It makes sense that businesses needed a rigid management structure to keep things running smoothly where managers often behaved as surrogate parent figures to very young workers, particularly in the days preceding child labor laws.

Today manufacturing accounts for 8.5 percent of all jobs, many of which will require a college education to run the robots that are now commonplace in manufacturing. Thirty-five percent of women have college degrees and 34 percent of men, a significant increase from 1950.

As industry has evolved to encompass more creative functions, employees have been required to possess greater levels of maturity and professionalism and deeper levels of thought. Despite this shift in our expectations of employees, the management structure in most businesses has not changed much since the manufacturing era. The parent-child dynamic that was established in a different time remains entrenched in work culture today. It is self-defeating; employees once needed structure to be effective in robotic execution; efficacy in today's workforce requires maturity, autonomy, and creativity. It is another factor driving the transition from the mechanical business philosophy to Adaptive.

Attention spans are also collapsing and with that the patience to wait for that big promotion; technologies make it easy to find that next job opportunity. No more circling opportunities in the classifieds section of the newspaper as I once did. Employees would rather quit and go to another company than stick it out for decades with their current employer. These people used to be labeled as job hoppers. Now it is commonplace for an employee to be with a company for just a few years (about four, according to the Bureau of Labor Statistics) before moving on. This number is trending downward. Gone are the days of a thirty-year career with a gold watch at the end.

In addition to rapidly changing workplace demographics, we are also seeing an explosion in powerful new machine-learning algorithms that herald a new industrial revolution for tasks once relegated to humans. Deep learning algorithms, also known as Convolutional Neural Networks (CNNs for short). can recognize cancer more effectively than humans, for example. I once led an R&D project that used CNNs to learn the behavior of human employees doing document cultivation work that nobody thought could be automated. The resulting solution proved to be more effective than humans, completing their task in hours rather than months. These same algorithms are at the heart of self-driving cars. In the legal field, an artificially intelligent system can act as an attorney and get people out of parking tickets.

If you perform a repetitive function in your job, a machine will soon be helping you with that.

It isn't just that machine-learning algorithms are becoming increasingly more powerful. Technology is becoming increasingly more accessible and far less expensive. AWS has everything necessary for a kid out of college to creatively destroy almost any business with extremely low up-front costs. Developers can get away with quite a lot before they break through the "free tier" that companies like AWS provide small businesses to get them going. Moreover, these powerful machine-learning algorithms are available as a configurable service in AWS. Finally, AWS is scalable, which means that a prototype running against a few hundred transactions can scale up to billions of transactions without any added effort—just cash. The implication is that if something is automatable, it soon will be, at scale, and for far less cost than the humans it will replace.

With these massive changes, the workforce will continue

to shift away from repetitive tasks and more toward positions requiring independent thought and creativity. These types of minds are inherently not going to thrive at the hands of hierarchical management, and business results will suffer as a result. They are increasingly demanding a different kind of workplace and a different organizational model. Their intellectual curiosity will demand continuous improvement and more frequent and sustainable acknowledgment of that progress. They do not want a boss; they want a coach who will help them level up to new opportunities.

These crazy kids with their long hair and rock 'n' roll music! GET OFF MY LAWN!!! How dare these whippersnappers expect a job they love, employed by a company focused on success, and working with colleagues dedicated to helping them level up their skills? Why, when I was their age, I was miserable in my work, and they should be too!

Of course, I am being facetious, but I've heard executives and leaders say these things while whining about the expectations of younger workers. To them I say that collaboration technologies and chatbots will only advance in their sophistication. These trends will not recede, only strengthen.

Each one of these tectonic shifts by itself is front-page news. To create the Adaptive model, I harnessed the power of these new collaboration technologies, wrapped them up in friendly, helpful, compassionately curious bots, and deployed them at scale through the communication backplane people were already using to get work done. This communication substrate enables developers to rapidly create and deploy bots that can augment every single person in a company. *That's a big deal!*

ORCHESTRATING COLLABORATION AT SCALE

What can we do with our shiny new collaboration platform and our army of bots? We can orchestrate collaboration and individual behavior in huge groups of people to solve massive problems and drive unprecedented change. Let's explore a few different patterns.

USING BOTS TO MANAGE TIME AND WORKLOAD

My wife's successful speech-therapy practice keeps her insanely busy. I happen to be an exercise nut who occasionally chides her for not exercising enough. Whenever I do, I find myself at the receiving end of a swift rebuke. Yet, when my wife's fitness watch tells her she should stand up and walk around, she stands up and walks around. There is something inherently less agitating about a bot suggesting you should do something good for you than a human telling you the same thing. Bots don't judge. People do, however, and that runs counter to empathy.

It is not just my wife; I have noticed this repeatedly. About halfway through my research into Adaptive, I realized that individual work discipline is critical for flat, fluid teams. This is where managers and project managers have historically played a crucial role in hierarchical organization models. They drive discipline, making sure all work is moving to closure as quickly and efficiently as possible. This is also the most robotic, and therefore least rewarding, part of their job. It is usually the greatest point of irritation between a manager and their direct reports, and where pointed complaints about micromanaging are most prevalent. I have felt this sting myself. No matter how talented my direct reports were, I always found myself hounding them to update an issue. This was not my favorite activity, and it set the tone for my relationship with everyone else on the team as the overbearing boss-man.

Upon realizing this, I decided to automate away as much of this function as I could. After six weeks of coding I had created an automated project administration bot. This bot was a taskmaster in a way I could never muster. Every day, without fail, this bot would review everyone's work, apply my heuristics and the heuristics of the team project managers, and then pester the team to better manage their work through the messaging platform we were using.

The effects were nothing short of astonishing. The first

thing that happened was that the bot found an unsettling number of issues with the way people were managing their work. Even with a pack of project managers and myself overseeing the work, it still found things that had been left to languish, the metaphorical equivalent of a basement filled with deferred decisions. The bot did not care what the excuse was, and its philosophy was always the same: fix it or I'll be back to pester you tomorrow. Whereas human managers don't have the robotic capacity to review everything and the constitution to chase down every problem, bots do.

Next, I built heuristics into the bot to help each person plan their day by helping them understand and prioritize their work. Humans are awful at time management, whereas bots are awesome at it. Each day, every person received a daily digest to help them figure out how to attack their tasks. On a few occasions I disabled the daily agenda for maintenance and then measured the effect it had and, sure enough, within about a week, work discipline degraded, and the bot found an increasing number of issues. When I turned the digest back on, the number of issues dropped within days.

The team loved it. In fact, team members loved it so much that the project manager moved on to different work as a business analyst. Think about that for a minute—a team member who had a depth of experience in the industry was freed from the yoke of robotic project administration work and was now free to pursue a more creative career. Having a bot automate the rote project administration work and drive work discipline had a massive impact. The team anthropomorphized the bot, whose name was Pepper (yes, a blatant Iron Man reference; don't judge me). People would post messages to Slack saying things like, "You need to update that issue. You don't want to piss off Pepper."

The impact on me was just as transformative. Suddenly, I wasn't the taskmaster—the bot was. Weirdly, even though the bot was behaving in the way I programmed it, any negative energy was transferred away from me and onto the bot. As a result, my relationship with the team changed, enabling me to accentuate my coaching role and de-emphasize my management role (aka, my robotic, confrontational role). It also freed up an immense amount of time and energy that I then converted into more bot development. I did not fully appreciate how much this low-value administrative overhead took out of me every day. The days of coming home and wondering what concrete value I had delivered were fading into the rearview mirror.

USING BOTS TO SCALE TRUST AND EMPATHY

Thrilled with the positive impact bots had on issues of

productivity, I decided to build a coaching bot, which is how I was able to scale empathy and trust. Here the effect was even more powerful, if nuanced. It turns out that chatbots are excellent facilitators. Remember when you were a kid and had a crush on someone? Of course, you couldn't just walk right up to that person and tell them you had a crush on them. That would be insanity! What if they rejected you? What if they laughed at you? No, the social judgment would be too great. Better to write a note and have a trusted friend deliver it.

It turns out we are all still in grade school because giving someone critical feedback is still socially awkward and socially risky. What if the person gets angry or you hurt their feelings? What if they don't see your point of view? No, the potential social humiliation is too great. Better to write a note and have a trusted bot deliver it. Even better if that bot has artificially intelligent tips for you to woo your love interest more effectively like a mechanical Casanova!

So, I built the bot to fan out across the company every quarter to ask people to provide feedback to their colleagues. It would collect that feedback, anonymize it, perform some analysis on it, then deliver the results to everyone, along with an aggregate analysis to the coaching team.

When I launched the coaching bot, I discovered that

people were far more willing to tell the bot their feedback and let it handle the social interaction than they were to give verbal or more traditionally written feedback—let alone face-to-face feedback! In fact, the change-management team I worked with initially insisted that we instead do only face-to-face for a quarter as a warm-up exercise. It was a disaster. When faced with mandatory meetings to share uncomfortable feedback, the people involved reverted to chatting about more comfortable topics like their kids, the weather, or the insanity of this crazy face-to-face idea.

I later enhanced the bot to coach people on how to give great feedback. By this point, I had collected a massive amount of written feedback and was able to search for correlations between features in the feedback and stronger individual improvement. Because this was a chatbot operating in the same messaging system everyone was using to get work done, the bot could interact naturally with each person to help them craft the most productive feedback possible based on its earlier language analysis. The result was an amazing amount of high-quality feedback that we could then mine for ways to improve both the relationships and the individuals who formed the social fabric of the team.

A unique aspect of this bot is that it works with each employee to supply great feedback and share it with the recipient only when the author is ready. This is opposed to a fire-and-forget survey. The author would write some feedback, the bot would tell them how they could improve it to achieve a better result, and the author and bot would repeat this cycle until the author was happy with the result.

In examining the log files, I discovered that the number of cycles dropped over time while the quality of the feedback continued to improve. I believe the reason for this is based on something called perceptual learning that I first learned about from software engineering legend and author Kathy Sierra. She discusses the seemingly impossible task of determining if a chick will grow up to be a hen (female) or rooster (male). Most of us can't look at a chick and at once tell if it will grow up to be a hen or a rooster, but some people can. The problem is that these people can't explain how they do it.

This is the infuriating thing about so many experts—we can't replicate their awesomeness because they can't explain why or how they are so awesome. I run into this regularly with my own development teams. After forty years in the R&D field, I instinctually see where roads will lead to absolute ruin or potential success. Granted, I am not perfect by any stretch of the imagination, but I'm right more often than I am wrong. To the great dismay of the teams I am coaching who ask me how I do it, my common refrain is, "I'm not exactly sure why; I can just tell you that my Spidey senses say so."

Kathy Sierra talks about an experiment done years ago and replicated many times since that can short-circuit expertise to, in her words, "make users awesome." The experiment goes like this: give a novice a box of chicks, position an expert behind them, and tell the novice to pick up a chick and make a guess. The expert will rapidly tell the novice if their guess is correct or not. With each guess, the novice gradually becomes an expert, one axonal adjustment at a time.

This is where bots are the killer application of organizational transformation. They are ever present within the collaboration platform and always available to users in need at the exact moment in which they are needed. This enables them to work as the expert standing over your shoulder, letting you know if you are correct or not. By building feedback expertise into the bot and giving it an opportunity to correct the user *in the moment*, it can quickly create feedback experts.

I first ran into this dynamic with a bot named Hubot from GitHub. The bot could shoulder the burden of tasks that were repetitive, and it was also hilarious. One of the things it tried to do was monitor conversations. When it detected what it felt were angry exchanges—specifically, ALL CAPS MESSAGES THAT MIGHT INDICATE ANGER—it would post pictures of manatees to calm everyone down. Who can be angry when looking at pictures of manatees? Despite the hilarity of the bot, it did regulate discussions. People learned to better regulate themselves in heated exchanges on Slack because they knew Hubot would call them out with manatees if they went nonlinear. Of course, whenever anyone wanted to see a manatee, they would POST SOMETHING IN ALL CAPS.

My dog Charlie does something similar. He is an empath disguised as a golden retriever. He can sense any negative emotion, like anxiousness, anger, agitation, or frustration, and then spring into action. Who can stay angry when an adorable retriever looks up at you from your lap with a look that says, "Dude, be chill"? Charlie has trained our entire family to stay calm, cool, and collected through perceptual learning. He is the family expert in being chill, and when we are not, he gives us a simple "no" in the exact moment to help us chicken-sex our way to a peaceable household.

So, this is the real power of chatbots and how they can scale empathy and trust. If you can devise a way to position them to correct or encourage a behavior with immediacy, compassion, and curiosity, then you can leverage the power of perceptual learning to teach everyone any number of lessons designed to create workplace nirvana.

USING BOTS FOR STRATEGIC ALIGNMENT

Finally, I decided to go for a moonshot—*using a bot to align each person with the overall company strategy.* Do you know what your company strategy is? What are you doing as an individual to drive it forward? During the Adaptive Experiment, I learned that when people understand their connection with the overall company strategy, they become engaged employees in a big, big way.

Most employees want to be part of something greater than themselves. Meanwhile, most companies have a tough time driving strategic vision down to individual execution. How can you align thousands of employees, each with their own agenda, with the company strategy? *Psssst...bots!*

Before the Adaptive Engagement Platform, the best approach I saw was at Perot Systems, where every employee had to align with a change initiative and explain how they were going to drive it forward. Perot had bought a platform designed to enable employees to align with the Perot strategy. This was way before its time and, unfortunately, there was no follow-up or human accountability. It was just another robotic exercise.

The bot, however, can reach out to every employee, get them to identify how they personally align with the strategy, and follow up with them regularly to see how things are going. The bot can even give them coaching advice along the way.

The impact was incredible. Even though the first implementation of this strategy alignment bot was rudimentary, the impact on team cohesiveness and engagement was powerful. I have since expanded on this early work to cultivate and leverage collaboration to drive continuous, sustainable, strategic execution at scale with every employee. Doing this manually would require an army of project managers and strategy consultants, and it still would have been too much. With collaboration technologies and bots, you can augment every single employee to be a strategy execution expert. The result is every executive's dream—the bot will ensure that every employee has an answer to the question, "What are you doing to drive the company strategy?"

NOW, FOR THE WARNING LABEL

Chatbots can also confuse matters and send the wrong message if you aren't careful with the language you use.

People anthropomorphized my bots because I designed them to operate like a character in a video game. I built a dialogue engine capable of sensing the situation the bots were in, and with that knowledge, the bot was able to pull out tailored language to direct the user in a productive way. I wanted to achieve a form of accountability equivalent to the social accountability found in human networks. I had seen this dynamic in video games, so why not with chatbots?

However, I soon realized that I was unqualified to construct this dialogue. I wasn't a psychologist, yet I was writing dialogue to achieve a psychological effect. What's more, I'm not a speech therapist, so what I was writing could be easily misunderstood in many circumstances. When I realized this, I promptly partnered with a psychologist and a speech therapist to help me with all the dialogue. The experience was eye-opening. When the psychologist and speech therapist reviewed my draft dialogue, they deemed it to be judgmental, not supportive, which explains why I saw an increase in judgmental behavior among the team!

The speech therapist and psychologist found a host of problems—including dialogue that had two interpretations or dialogue with unintended psychological effects. There was dialogue that could be misinterpreted and cause negative side effects! YIKES! I didn't intend for any of these things to happen, and the experience revealed to me just how careful you must be with chatbot language.

Language can be a powerful, blunt instrument. Think about how quickly the comments section on a news article can get out of hand. Think about Twitter flame wars. One person is linguistically bashing a person with the sharpest tools they have in that moment—the written word. Before long, one person is accusing the other of being a Nazi, also known as Godwin's Law.

When you are speaking with someone in person, facial expressions and body language supply vast amounts of information and increase the chances that the other person will understand you. Take away that information, and the chances they will fully understand you drop precipitously.

Psychologists and speech therapists helped make the bot dialogue much more beneficial. We use every interaction with the user as an opportunity to scale empathy and trust as well as create positive energy. This could be everything from a dialogue used to coach the user on writing great feedback all the way down to language used in a button designed to generate positive energy. Because the bots deploy this powerful dialogue in the exact moment that it is needed, entire companies can begin chicken-sexing their way to workplace nirvana.

CHAPTER FOUR

FIXING WHAT'S BROKEN

———

The mechanical business philosophy is showing its age and will continue to get worse. Every time I speak with a startup founder, it becomes more obvious. A new way of getting work done is already emerging thanks to collaboration technologies and bot-augmented teams. Rather than fighting the tide, we need to harness it. To harness these emerging changes, we must first acknowledge them and recognize that they will only accelerate.

Adaptive organizations use self-determination for employees augmented by bots working in a robust collaboration platform to move fast and beat the competition. Companies like these can quickly crowdsource new collaborative patterns to achieve continuous, sustainable, and strategic change to solve massive problems.

There are things you must do to get ready for this kind

of fluidity or you won't reap the full benefit and could even be counterproductive. Deploying Slack or Teams can be damaging if done improperly. Deploying irritating bots can quickly create a backlash. People often look for every excuse to avoid change and stay with what they know. Let's walk through some of the concrete changes necessary to begin the transformation to a bot-enabled Adaptive business.

BEHAVIORAL DEFAULTS

In the mechanical business philosophy, employees are like baby elephants chained to a stake in the ground. They learn they can't go anywhere, so even when they grow to adulthood and develop more than enough power to tear that stake out of the ground, it never occurs to them that they have the power to set themselves free. The same is true for employees tethered by their reporting line and robotic processes.

In *Originals: How Non-Conformists Move the World*, author Adam Grant writes about two kinds of employees—those who change their working defaults and those who do not. Some employees challenge the default working assumptions and try several ways of doing something, while others merely follow whatever they've been told. Being a nonconformist, I have a lot of experience with this.

The org chart sends a clear message that your place is here, and you must earn your way out of it by pleasing your boss. It is a daily reminder of who controls your paycheck. That's the stake you're chained to. Personal circumstances amplify this positional power; for example, a single parent may think twice about pushing boundaries, even if doing so would result in a net benefit to the company. The father of a special-needs child who gets paid to do what his manager tells him to will do exactly that and no more.

Over the years, I've encountered dozens of wickedly smart people who see a better path forward but won't say a word. The stakes are too high for them. The rules of the road are clearly stated in their title, their station in the org chart, and the person they report to. The box we are repeatedly told to think outside of is the box our company has put us in.

Herein lies the essential difference between hierarchies and Adaptive. Whereas hierarchies are all about command and control by the elite few, Adaptive revolves around self-determination enabled by empathy, trust, accountability, and empowerment for everyone. In such an environment, employees no longer work inside a box created by a company, but instead are bubbles of influence that are as big as they can make them through results demonstrated to their colleagues and facilitated by bots.

Let's start with some organizational behaviors you will want to begin changing to begin to untether your employees to create a great amount of autonomy that will enable you to move faster, get more from your employees, and become more Adaptive.

TRUST

Research shows repeatedly that trust is the number-one building block of any successful company. In his seminal book *5 Dysfunctions of a Team*, Patrick Lencioni writes that without trust, there will be a fear of conflict. Without trust, there can be no debate about a better way forward. In the absence of that debate, what are you going to do? Exactly what your manager tells you to do, because that is what their manager told them to do, and so on up the chain.

In *The SPEED of Trust: The One Thing That Changes Everything* by Stephen M. R. Covey, the author explains that in the absence of trust everything takes longer because you must check and verify everything. There is a grain of sand on the beach for every time I've seen this dynamic in play. This kind of power play is most commonly seen in workplace politics by way of the manner in which people use the email carbon copy (aka CC) field on a judgmental email to a fellow employee and the inherently evil blind carbon copy (aka BCC) field. People use the CC to copy a manager to exert positional power by proxy, indirectly tattling on someone to their manager. People use the BCC to do this in a form of subterfuge. And while inboxes are filling up with such emails, trust is rapidly decaying, email threads grow and grow, and, most of all, very rarely does any of this result in real value for the company.

In an Adaptive business, on the other hand, trust is essential. With trust comes autonomy—employees who can move rapidly on their own without being centrally controlled and guided by nudges from bots. This level of self-determination explains why engagement scores are so starkly different between a mechanical business and an Adaptive one.

Even though most of us want self-determination as human beings, in practice it is still exceedingly difficult to break through the entrenched behaviors of the corporate environment. This isn't just an American problem; my research uncovered that breaking through this mindset is the biggest issue across many countries, and with employees of various ages and cultural backgrounds. Across the board, one of the most difficult hurdles to overcome in moving closer to an Adaptive organization is getting employees to the point where they can rediscover their self-determination within the work environment, and that requires trust. This is where bots can be tremendously helpful.

By putting bots in place as facilitators and coaches,

employees can supply feedback and updates to one another in ways that build trust. The bots are the trusted confidant you can turn to for advice on how to tell your colleague that they have room for improvement. The bots are your trusty sidekick that will at once tell you if an update you just wrote comes across as snarky and then help you understand the impact of that.

To get ready for this brave new world, your company must emphasize trust. Bring in training if you can afford it, or read some of the books I've mentioned above if you cannot. Regardless of how you do it, make the change obvious and do not ever backslide. The fastest way to sow distrust is by making trust an imperative and then not following through. Doing so will yield one step forward and two steps back.

INTEGRITY

Low-integrity behaviors can lead to employees trying to discern the hidden agenda so they can use it to their benefit. We see this hypocrisy in the way many companies promote staff members. If a higher position, such as executive vice president, opens, many companies will hire from the outside instead of promoting from within. This can happen because either most companies don't trust their own employees to rise to new levels or the company hasn't invested in growing them to excel in such a position. Occasionally this can be because the damage created by an internal competition for a senior position would be too great, pointing to a whole host of other issues. Instead, they hire individuals who are slotted to play a role in the hierarchy. In other words, most companies don't hire people to grow; they hire them to fill a function without much thought for cultivating them to supply added value to the company in the longer term.

Companies do this despite their adamant statements to the contrary. They declare their desire to support the growth of their employees, but when it comes to promoting into positions of significant power, they often look outside the company. This creates a disconnect between messaging and actual behavior, which in turn creates a low-integrity relationship between company and employee.

To make matters worse, pay raises are often not based on merit but on an employee's relationship with their manager. Since a single individual is usually making pay increase decisions, raises often come down to how much a manager likes an employee, which can be independent of actual business results.

Companies with integrity measure an employee's value by their sphere of influence as measured by their team, not just by their manager. As employees gain new skills and use them to move the company strategy forward, their team rewards them with more opportunities and the company compensates them in a way that recognizes the value of their skills in the market. None of this requires title changes, job requisitions, CFO signatures, etc. Yet we torture ourselves with the administrative overhead of this system when all anyone really wants is fair, high-integrity recognition for the value they provide. Below I write about a specific practice to do this very thing.

Integrity suffers most egregiously during the termination process. I find it perennially befuddling that companies spend so much time standardizing and perfecting their hiring processes to proactively find great employees, but then their termination processes are entirely reactionary. It is as though we are surprised every time that we need to stop employment for an underperforming resource. Even worse, the decision to fire someone is based entirely on one person's opinion—the manager.

We often say that work isn't a popularity contest. "I'm not here to make friends; I'm here to win." Based on my unscientific review of people who use this line, they never win! In his book *The No Asshole Rule,* Robert Sutton explains in detail why this is the case. Jerks try to increase their sphere of influence along one vector (IQ), to the exclusion of others (EQ). So work *is* a popularity contest, and harnessing this fact can drive business results if done in good faith. What often happens, though, is that the only popularity that counts is with the manager. This can lead to "protected employees." The manager likes them, but often their colleagues do not. Their protected status often deepens the dislike by colleagues because of the inherent injustice in the dynamic.

Here's an example: I once worked for a company that acquired another, older company. Shortly after the buyout, one of the acquired company's most impressive employees quit. During his exit interview—designed to assess legal exposures—we asked him if he felt he'd ever been discriminated against.

"Well, hell, yes I do!" he replied, much to the HR manager's surprise. He explained how a coworker used to give him menacing looks in meetings, cursing him under his breath because of his religious beliefs.

HR decided to launch an investigation. An HR representative, let's call her Lisa, went to the employee's office and discovered a bunch of ceremonial swords, religious artifacts, and a statue of a naked man engulfed in flames. Seeing the investigation from across the hallway, another employee said, "I see you found the statue."

"You knew about this?" Lisa asked incredulously.

"Of course," the employee replied. "He's been displaying that stuff for years."

"Why did management tolerate this?" she asked.

"Don't ask me," he said. "I just work here." The mantra of the disengaged employee.

Lisa assumed that for this to have persisted, the employee displaying the oddities must have been good at his job. When she researched his files, though, she learned he was terrible. He was often absent. He did bizarre things like walking to work barefoot—in the snow—for a year. But manager after manager tolerated the behavior, so it continued until the acquiring company fired him. Why did each manager tolerate the terrible behavior? Because the person's *original* manager really liked him, despite his weird behavior and poor business results, and the pattern just continued. This is a prime example of low-integrity behavior by those in positions of power. I'll come back to this when we explore practice later on.

TRANSPARENCY

Another key to Adaptive is transparency. Mature, skilled workers desire it. Younger workers demand it. My twelve-year-old daughter collaborates with her robotics team using Slack—not because I told her to, but because she

Googled, "How can I be more transparent with my team?" Kids today.

Transparency should be consistent, beginning when potential candidates first log on to your company website. It is this full transparency that will ensure the right people are drawn to your company—and, believe me, they will be. The type of people you need to build your Adaptive organization will beat down your door when they see a transparent company. These are people who want to collaborate, grow, and be a *part* of something that adds more to their lives than just a paycheck.

Many companies aren't ready for the transparency collaboration that technologies afford. Most companies implicitly tell employees, "*You* can't handle the truth," and they reinforce the tired parent-child relationship most managers have with their employees. I always find it ironic when companies treat their employees like children and then accuse those same employees of childish behavior. If information can be shared, it should be shared with qualified people (or bots) on hand to help employees work through any implications. Of course, there is some information that cannot be shared because it may run afoul of the law or tip off a competitor. But there is little information that *must* be kept from employees.

When I suggest that some companies infuse this level

of transparency into their culture through collaboration technologies, they argue that they do not want to distract employees from their duties with information that could be disruptive. When I hear this, I respond, "Do you really think you can keep a secret anymore?" Rumors spread quickly, and company rumors are damaging because they are often a caricature of the truth. It's better to share the information so you can control the message. My second response is, "What, you don't think your employees are already distracted?" Between smartphones, breaking news alerts on their smartwatches, and the regular human interaction in any office (especially open office plans), employees are already distracted. It is better to distract them with frank information delivered with sincerity than for them to be blindsided or obsessed with trying to find out whether a rumor is true.

Transparency enables employees to move autonomously and without hesitation because they have all of the data they need to ensure they don't zig when they should have zagged. Furthermore, they aren't forced to rely on the "information keepers" (managers) before making decisions. Transparency is also an extension of trust while opaqueness is an extension of mistrust. Without transparency, self-determination and new organizational models are impossible.

FACILITATING DISCUSSIONS OVER RULING BY EDICT

In a mechanical business, there isn't a requirement for debate. The manager uses their positional power to set the direction, and everyone executes according to those directions, even when they think the directions are a terrible idea. Collaboration technologies create more dynamic workplaces where influence is the primary currency. Collaboration technologies have no hierarchy, lending themselves to flat organizations.

Adaptive organizations instead use social networks to get to the best ideas instead of relying on one person to rule by edict. By leveraging the social network, you tap into the intelligence and knowledge within a web of relationships. To do this, however, requires very careful facilitation.

In his book *Creativity, Inc.: Overcoming the Unseen Forces That Stand in the Way of True Inspiration*, Pixar CEO Ed Catmull describes a similar strategy. Pixar organized a group that they referred to as a brain trust—a group of people who have played a major hand in making some of the greatest movies the planet has ever known. When a team needs to decide which direction a movie should go, Pixar's brain trust steps in to help.

When I attempted to implement a model similar to the Pixar brain trust, what I found was positional power all over again. People who were in the brain trust were authorities on some subject and were unwittingly wielding their power by making subjective statements of fact. For example, "I think what you should do is..." The moment they did this, everyone fell back into common dysfunctions. Brains would simply shut down because the person receiving the advice heard, "Thou shalt do this." Who is going to be stupid enough to go against the brain trust?

The moment this dysfunction appears, everyone just missed an opportunity to learn how to organize in new ways. The recipient of the advice lost out on a moment to practice critical thinking skills. The leader missed an opportunity to help that person level up. Everyone might have missed an angle to a better solution.

The easiest solution is for managers to stop making work assignments. Instead, they should observe, ask open-ended questions first and leading questions second, teach, and do everything in their power to help employees become more autonomous and less tethered to that stake that tells them they are powerless.

PREPARE FOR CHANGE

Now that you understand the ways in which your company's mindset, ethos, and behaviors must shift to adopt Adaptive, it's time to start talking about what implementation will look like in terms of concrete practices.

CHAPTER FIVE

THE GOLDEN STRAITJACKET

In his book *The World Is Flat*, Thomas Friedman argues that economic prosperity will come to those countries that implement practices that force them to give up some sovereignty. He refers to this as the "Golden Straitjacket." Similarly, staying competitive in the modern age requires that you implement certain practices that cause you to relinquish positional power, which is effectively sovereignty over your piece of corporate turf.

Depending on where your company is in its journey, these changes might feel like a deal-breaker. But you can put the practices into place over time, moving at the speeds your competitors allow. As you introduce collaboration platforms and augment your teams with bots, they will evolve from the mechanical business philosophy to an Adaptive one naturally and without any additional help. In fact, one of the reasons I authored this book is because

I saw so many companies going through this transformation without realizing it and the results were not what they could have been.

Most workplaces can quickly infuse some elements of Adaptive to achieve greater fluidity and the ability to deal with rapid change. Certain departments within a company might move to Adaptive quickly while others keep a more traditional organization.

For example, creative divisions of your company might incorporate Adaptive elements at once and to profound effect. They will relish bots taking over rote tasks. My experience is that creative types are often horrendous at this kind of work anyway. Other functional areas may require robotic precision for tasks that are not automatable yet. Perhaps they aren't yet using a platform with a robust application programming interface (API) that a bot can access. Finance is a good example. Whenever you come across this kind of situation, you should at once begin looking for ways to remediate the situation and automate where you can.

Establishing an Adaptive model in your company is not an all-or-nothing endeavor. And it can't be rolled out overnight. Instead, it should be gradually employed so that your team has time to adjust, adapt, and build empathy and trust with their colleagues in the new system and find their place in it. Produce a strategy and then execute against the strategy using bots to orchestrate that execution.

So, with the behavioral changes in place from the earlier chapter, you are now ready to don the Golden Straight Jacket. Your employees are now psychologically prepared for greater autonomy and able to support more fluid and complex collaboration patterns. Now let's talk about specific methods to begin orchestrating these new patterns at scale.

DOCUMENT YOUR CULTURE

A key practice to increasing the autonomy needed for more complex collaboration patterns is keeping a well-documented culture. Having a well-documented culture that people believe in and follow gives everyone more autonomy than if you must look to your manager for cultural norms. Even if your company embraces the mechanical business philosophy, a culture document will lead to smoother operation by more autonomous employees. This established culture prevents individuals in positions of power from dictating the company culture according to their whims and preferences.

A well-documented culture empowers employees to refer to something more durable than an individual manager.

As we discussed earlier, a cultural narrative that does not hinge upon a single person, such as a manager or executive, prevents the whipsaw effect when characters leave the company. The culture is part of your company's legacy value; it survives regardless of who comes or goes and is something that investors can buy into that is more reliable than a mercurial leader.

Unfortunately, most companies communicate their culture in the form of "mouse-pad values"—company values printed on mouse pads and handed out to employees. As if seeing these values on a mouse pad will somehow change the culture. Imagine if you converted those values into strange alien runes that nobody could understand. That is the effect you achieve with this approach. The problem is that these values are often context-free. Employees can't connect their work life to the company values because they have a tough time seeing opportunities to apply them in their daily work life.

The alternative is what I refer to as a cultural narrative. I saw this from the company Valve in the form of their now-famous employee handbook. This handbook was a story where new employees could imagine themselves as the hero. Instead of mouse-pad values, Valve communicated their company values in the form of parables that enabled new employees to visualize their working lives in archetypes the company saw as valuable to high-performing teams.

Yes, writing a cultural narrative is initially more labor intensive than holding a one-day session to banter about values and then ordering mouse pads. I encourage you to find someone savvy in crafting short stories and then work with them to help you craft your narrative. The payoff in the long run will far exceed the modest investment up front.

When you document your culture in the form of a narrative, employees can refer to parables from the narrative to guide their behavior in ways most productive to the company. Because everyone is working from those same parables, you can achieve far greater autonomy and speed.

COLLABORATION PLATFORM

Not surprisingly, the single biggest thing you can do to create an Adaptive organization is to implement a messaging collaboration platform like Slack or Teams. Collaboration platforms enhance the fluidity your company needs to stay competitive. They also provide autonomous employees with the means to rapidly crowd-source new organizational designs to tackle bigger and bigger problems, aided by bots.

If you take away just one thing from this book, I would like it to be this: these collaboration platforms will soon be table stakes to staying competitive. They will save you the time and expense spent on meetings, reduce collaboration friction, and enable you to deploy bot sidekicks to aid your employees in automating rote tasks and getting back to more human work.

Despite the critical nature of collaboration platforms, tackle culture first; the platform will be a conduit through which team members support and strengthen the culture. Throughout the Adaptive Experiment, people used the platform to publicly point out when a decision was inconsistent with our culture. This signals that people are operating on their own within a culture they trust.

Some people may blanch at adding another tool to the company tool chain, but this type of platform helps shrink that chain. The number of powerful integrations for many technologies is rapidly expanding. With a collaboration platform that emphasizes the strength of their API, you can begin to cut down on the number of technologies people need to know about. Instead, they can access those same technologies through the collaboration platform.

WHAT TO LOOK FOR IN A
COLLABORATION PLATFORM

The minimum characteristics I counsel my clients to look for in a platform include these:

- It must be ubiquitous. Everyone in the company will eventually have access to it.

- It must enable individuals to crowdsource new channels at will (and delete them when they are no longer needed). You will want to have some control in the beginning so that you can shape the evolution, but after that early point the channels should belong to the tribe.

- It must sport a robust API so you can plug in bots.

- It should have a rich, rapidly expanding bot marketplace. Ideally, a bot will already integrate with your work-management system.

- It should have extensive online documentation to support bot development, such as Stackoverflow.com.

- It should have a great desktop, mobile, and web client to enable team members to jack into whatever access method works for them in whatever context they find themselves.

- It should be easy to integrate with it. This will become critical as you look to deploy applications and bots.

- The platform should support easy guest access so that you can work with outside vendors and partners.

- It should support your company's information governance and security standards. Without this, your security team will be very leery of a shiny new collaboration tool.

- Users should love it. Give team members the opportunity to give it a whirl and make themselves at home on the platform before making a purchasing decision. This will replace email as their primary mode of written communication.

THE LOGISTICS

Your company may balk at the cost of a collaboration platform, but studies have shown these platforms can save money by reducing time in meetings and breaking down silos. None of those studies included the financial implications of bots, which, in my experience, are low-cost sponges for high-cost work. But, more importantly, they build and strengthen relationships among employees, and you can measure that impact using social network analyses helped by bots.

Once you identify the right platform, develop a comprehensive rollout strategy. The details of this strategy are beyond the scope of this book, although I have written about it more extensively on my LinkedIn (https://www.linkedin.com/in/chris-creel-827ba4/).

Most collaboration platform rollouts fail because the company doesn't put a communication strategy in place. These platforms are deceptively easy to use, but don't do what many companies do—throw the technology at their workforce and walk away. At the end of the rollout, you want your employees to be enthusiastic about the collaboration platform and have the information they need to use it in creative ways. Support that creativity instead of squelching it, because this is the beginning of creating new complex collaboration patterns.

WORK DISCIPLINE

Work-management platforms like Jira and GitHub are critical to Adaptive because they enable employees to manage their own work, rather than a manager. Bots can then work with employees on their work discipline while absorbing the rote work from project administrators and project managers. Excellent work-management systems also support transparency and, when used properly, can foster competition around work-discipline excellence. More on this below.

Work-management systems have evolved in recent years, creating an explosion of high-quality platforms that help companies manage work at an enterprise scale. The idea behind these systems is simple: anytime an employee works on something, they log their progress in the system so everyone is on the same page.

I encourage you to choose your work-management platform and collaboration platform at the same time to ensure they work seamlessly together. For example, employees should be able to create an issue for someone in the work-management system through a bot operating in the collaboration platform. Likewise, if someone's work discipline begins to degrade, a bot should reach out to them in the collaboration platform to help them.

WHAT TO LOOK FOR IN A WORK-MANAGEMENT PLATFORM

I tell my clients to look for qualities in a work-management platform that are remarkably similar to those they should look for in a collaboration platform. Those include the following:

- It must be ubiquitous. Everyone in the company will eventually have access to it.

- It must sport a robust API so you can plug in bots.

- It should have extensive online documentation of active forum activity on sites like Stackoverflow.com.

- It should have a great desktop, mobile, and web client to enable team members to jack into whatever access method works for them in whatever context they find themselves.

- It should be easy to integrate with it. This will be critical when you deploy applications and bots.

- It should have a rich portfolio of applications that integrate with it and can aid your employees.

- It should support easy guest access so you can easily work with outside vendors and partners.

- It should support your company's information governance and security standards.

- Users should love it.

For this, you will need a rollout strategy that dovetails with the rollout of your collaboration platform. Work-management systems are harder to deploy than collaboration platforms because they demand an investment in administrative overhead. This benefits the organization but not necessarily the individual. Collaboration platforms, on the other hand, give everyone something they need—the ability to quickly get things done by working with colleagues. There is an almost immediate return on investment if they are fun to use.

When developing your strategy, try to incentivize use of the work-management system. Just telling everyone to use it won't cut it. Bots can foster adoption. For example, I built a bot for the Adaptive Engagement Platform that created a work-discipline leaderboard to help employees see how their work discipline compared to their colleagues. This created healthy competition among individuals to stay off the bottom of the board. I created another leaderboard that compared the velocity of different strategy change initiatives, which created a healthy competition among teams to capture their work and move it across their board. Finally, the automated project administrator I built for the Adaptive Engagement Platform monitored workloads. When it detected a possible overload, it alerted the person who created the issue and asked them to reconsider the assignment or due date. All these things were designed to gamify work discipline and train employees how to improve.

Finally—and this will be counterintuitive—*don't go crazy.*

I've seen work-management systems used as an executive bludgeon to beat people with rather than as a productivity tool to offload repetitive work. Something about these work-management systems taps into the mechanical business philosophy in such a visceral way that things can get out of hand quickly. To blunt this effect, I encourage you to roll out your management system incrementally and, at each step, to ask yourself, "Is this making people's lives better and the workplace more fluid?" If the answer is no, jump back into your collaboration platform and elicit feedback on how to continue.

VIDEO CONFERENCING

All of the research shows that remote employees are more productive than employees in an office. During the Adaptive Experiment, I had tremendous success creating global R&D teams entirely composed of remote employees.

Video conferencing is a critical tool to create trust and empathy from a distance. If you can, choose one that can be easily launched from your collaboration platform. That way people can chat with one another and, in case it becomes clear they need a face-to-face, easily launch the video-conferencing solution. Some collaboration platforms have a video-conferencing solution built into them.

FLATTENING THE ORGANIZATION

Once you have these critical pieces in place, you are on your way to creating an Adaptive business. These solutions melt rigid teams and create more fluidity while scaling trust and empathy without explicit intervention.

In fact, once these pieces are in place, it might be a good time to pause. These new systems will cause a lot of changes in your company, so sit back, observe, ask questions, and experiment. These platforms provide new data and insights into how your company operates. Your org chart may remain the same, but the organizational network analysis will change as these new tools, practices, and behaviors take hold.

Once everyone is comfortable with this new relationship-centric technology stack, move on to the next step: flattening your organization.

I have spoken with companies that place as many as thirteen layers between an employee and the CEO. This means there are thirteen layers of people managing things and not contributing concrete output for the organization. This does not maximize production; it generates paperwork, meetings, and confusion—and that is the best-case scenario.

I don't recommend throwing away titles completely.

Instead, transition away from bestowing titles based on status and toward awarding titles based on what skills a person has. As you make that transition, get rid of as many layers as possible. This will give your company greater fluidity to tackle sudden changes in the market, workforce, and technology. When a company has too many titles, coworkers can fall into competitions and territorial behaviors that interfere with productivity, smart growth, and efforts to adopt an Adaptive mentality.

Flat organizations focus on contribution to the strategy rather than control over territory. How can each individual best contribute to the team's effort to drive output? This strategy gives employees a stronger voice. Everyone will sense how they can contribute, and that expands the skillsets a company has access to. Conversations that would have been clashes, now become negotiations or collaboration.

Many companies give lip service to flattening their organization, but most fail to achieve it. Deep hierarchies are often a symptom of a serious structural disease. For example, companies with weak culture need hierarchy because they lack a common operating system. Consequently, these companies feel they need tight control over individual behaviors, creating a destructive cycle. Maintaining the org chart requires tremendous administration, and the volume of work requires layers of management to distribute that burden. If companies can remove that administrative overhead or automate with bots, they can develop an inspiring cultural narrative. A flatter organization suddenly seems within easy reach.

The biggest hurdle is designing a mechanism for elevating personal status in a way that drives strategy-aligned execution instead of title-driven self-service. Since many people don't want to give up the titles that have been conferred upon them, consider naming functional categories, such as finance, human resources, development, DevOps, and operations. These should reflect the broad areas of interest that people typically pursue.

Then, create a skills catalog that lists all the critical skills your company feels it needs to compete within the event horizon of the company strategy. This skills catalog doesn't have to be comprehensive, and it will be fluid, ebbing and flowing alongside your evolving company strategy. To be more blunt—the skills catalog for 2019 will be different from the skills catalog for 2020, 2021, etc.

With the skills catalog in place, present opportunities for people to acquire and demonstrate these skills to better support the company strategy. As they do so, cheer like crazy. Give them some formal recognition of their newly demonstrated skills. A friend of mine who used to work in the military gave out custom-made tokens. Another friend gave out stickers that people stuck to their laptops. The recognition doesn't have to be big; it just has to happen. This gives employees a new way to level up their game and receive recognition. What's more, the recognition can be more frequent than the limited opportunities for promotion.

While there are lots of ways individual contributors win when flattening your org in this way, there is one potential loser: managers. When you flatten an organization, you are, by definition, saying that a group that used to be managed within a level will now be part of a larger group without positional power. So, what do you do with a manager who will no longer have direct reports? They could, obviously, become an individual contributor again. I've seen this happen successfully on at least a few occasions. They could become a coach (a specialized form of individual contributor), and that is something I've also seen happen a few times. Ideally, however, you want both—a manager who can contribute directly *and* parlay their management experience into coaching. One thing that can help figure out the best path forward is an organizational network analysis, which we will cover later.

Regardless, it should be obvious that the more hierarchical your organization, the more restrictions you face to creating new and novel organizational patterns.

PROMOTIONS

At many companies, promotions are rare and come with minor changes in station or pay. Some employees who may deserve a promotion won't get it because the next step up is already occupied, and that manager isn't going anywhere. Even if that manager leaves, companies often opt to hire outside because of a lack of investment in existing employees. If one manager is not good enough to progress up the ladder, everyone beneath them is stuck. It is just a crazy system! No wonder so many people leave a company to get "promoted" to the position that they feel reflects their talent. Of course, the cycle will just repeat itself at the next company, and nobody is the better for it.

However, the skill-acquisition movement is well underway, with companies like Udemy and Khan Academy leading the charge. Employees, especially younger ones, are often learning something in one of these platforms. Companies have caught on and are trying to make use of these platforms, but my sense is that there is still a lot of room for improvement.

The Adaptive way is to be proactive about the skills that will be necessary to achieve the company strategy. Bots can help each person figure out what those skills are, where they can be acquired (e.g., Udemy), and then orchestrate skill acquisition. Individuals can then acquire those skills using whatever method the company has accredited. Those skills have market value, so figure out what that value is ahead of time and make *that* your promotion. When someone acquires one of those skills and can put it to use in service of the company, announce it like you would any other promotion.

Think about the dynamic this sets up. First, instead of a one-dimensional promotion track (up the hierarchy), employees can instead pursue a multidimensional landscape based on their own interests and passions, yet all in service of the company strategy. Instead of getting "Peter principled," or promoted beyond their skillset, employees are now simply acquiring specific skills that have been named as necessary strategy execution. Instead of coworkers feeling jealousy toward someone who may or may not deserve a promotion, people instead see their colleagues getting ahead by acquiring strategically important skills. Rather than categorizing employees, they are tagged with skill badges.

This concept is how skill trees work inside of popular role-playing games like *World of Warcraft* and *Skyrim*. In these games people choose the skill pool that interests them most (such as elf, wizard, paladin, or thief). The skill pools then have different skill trees in which they can level up (archery, alchemy, spells, swords, etc.), depending on what they want to do in the game.

Now imagine something like this in the work environment. Choose a skill pool, such as strategy or initiative execution; think about the skills necessary to drive strategy execution in the coming quarter; and let the bots orchestrate the collaboration required to make it happen. Each of these skills will have some market value and can therefore serve as a way for employees to increase their base salary in small increments as they gain new skills in service to the strategy.

This model is sometimes referred to as "pay-for-performance." Some companies are getting rid of merit increases entirely and instead switching to just pay-for-performance. The idea is compelling because these pay increases can happen at any time in response to an employee who has leveled up their game in service to the company strategy. If you have a well-defined strategy with a list of the skills necessary for success, that serves as a far more effective incentive platform than the current merit-increase process.

For example, I once worked with a company that had made the decision to migrate large swaths of infrastructure to AWS to reduce infrastructure costs as part of their strategy for the coming year. This obviously required that the company build up AWS skills quickly. We named the list of AWS professional certifications that would be critical for this transition and told everyone about the skills that were of strategic importance. If they wanted to help drive the AWS change initiative, step one was getting the AWS professional certification. This certification is incredibly difficult to obtain, requiring many hours of study and a proctored exam. Meanwhile, we hired a consulting company that already had those skills and could accelerate the move while employees hit the books.

As people began trickling in with their AWS professional certification, we would cheer, hoot, and holler over an achievements channel in our collaboration platform. Taking a page out of Ross Perot's book, an executive would call the person to thank them for acquiring a strategically important skill. Finally, we added the market value of that certification to the person's annual salary. No promotions necessary, just new skills, new opportunities, and financial recognition. Now *that's* high integrity.

Here is another example. A friend of mine works for a company with a serious dedication to leadership that puts volunteers through a series of Harvard Business School leadership courses taught by a Harvard professor. My friend took some of these courses and excelled. At the end of the series of courses, her company held a graduation celebration and gave everyone a certificate and an iPad. The CEO personally thanked them for their hard work. They also adjusted the graduates' pay to recognize their newly earned skills. Wow, that's high integrity too.

When I explain this new promotion model to companies, one of the most frequent questions I hear in response is "What if we invest in someone and they leave?" Well, as Peter Baeklund once said, "What if we don't and they stay?"

So how can a bot orchestrate this pattern of collaboration? The employee chooses something they think they need to work on to better execute the strategy. Then, they choose an "accountability partner" or coach who will hold them accountable for acquiring and then demonstrating a new skill. Maybe they don't know who a suitable coach might be, and so the bot would facilitate finding one for them. Once they have a coach, then the bot will facilitate a discussion between the coach and employee throughout the process of acquiring the new skill. The bot can then monitor the discussion and provide tips to improve the relationship. This approach can scale to every employee.

MERIT INCREASES

Even if switching to a pay-for-performance model is not in the cards, I still encourage you to rethink the merit-increase process. In most companies, a manager receives a bucket of money based on the financial performance of the company and pay ranges for the employees in that manager's functional area. In good years that bucket is bigger, and in bad years it can be smaller. That is how merit increases are determined.

The manager handles distributing money solely based on their opinion. This is a raw, visceral, positional power play, and one that can do more damage than anything else. When one person is solely responsible for determining whether you can pay for your child's private-school education next year, you will always ask, "How high?" when told to jump.

By now you will not be surprised to learn that you can use a bot to calculate merit increases. If the bot is collecting feedback, supporting employees with their development objectives, and connecting this all to strategy, then the bot has all the necessary information to provide clear guidance to compensation boards. This bot can take all the coaching feedback provided to each employee for a given year into account and automatically recommend a merit increase. It also figures in the employee's geographic location in the world and the amount of total money available to cover the merit increases of all employees.

The key here is to make the entire algorithm available to everyone on the team. I even went as far as to make the code for the compensation bot available to everyone who wanted to review it (which ended up revealing few bugs). That's right, no more surprises when it comes to raises. Every employee should be able to download a model of the algorithm in the form of a spreadsheet to help determine their expected merit increase. Did they have a good or bad quarter? Did they learn new skills? If so, what is the market value of those skills? If they disagree with the algorithm, they can discuss it with someone. In my experience, this single system changes the dynamic of a team.

For example, one year a particularly promising engineer had a rough introduction to the team. He struggled to overcome years of institutional training to serve his manager rather than his colleagues. He still felt that rope tied to his leg. His performance flagged and the team felt it but were rooting for him because he had a lot of potential. Based on this, the model recommended the lowest possible merit increase. I was beside myself with anxiety over a meeting I was to have with him about the increase. However, when we met to discuss the news, he said, "Yeah, I already knew. I had plugged my numbers into the model. It was a fair assessment. I'm going to crush it this year, though!" And he did. The next year he pulled off the highest merit increase possible.

I am often asked, "Won't people game the model?" Well, people are already gaming the current model, so it makes sense that they will game this model as well. The key difference is that one game is far more productive for the company than the other. One game works to the sole benefit of the manager, while the other game helps the entire company.

That said, my response to this question is that in my six years of running the Adaptive Experiment, I never once saw an instance of people gaming the system. I think a key reason for this is that the transparency of the model and the simple mathematics that underpin it modulate low-integrity behavior. It is hard to hide in a network, and people are repelled by rewarding inferior performance, even if they have a tacit, in-kind agreement. This is not to say that people won't try to game the system. It is to say that their attempt will be hard to cover up because now everyone will be able to clearly see who they are.

ANNUAL REVIEWS

Annual evaluations provide staff with the opportunity to grow, expand, and adjust when necessary. It lets them know where they stand and where they should go to move the company forward. It also opens the avenue for salary increases and more responsibility.

The problem is, who can remember what happened over the last year? Today, it seems like enough happens in a week to fill up an entire year's worth of time in 1950. Furthermore, most managers aren't close enough to a person's work to supply an appropriate assessment of their skills. The annual review is a raw form of positional power, appointing one person and one person only with the authority to grant or deny a salary merit increase.

Adaptive has an answer for this, too. Bots aid employees by helping them write 360-degree reviews every quarter. As I wrote about earlier, I built bots that helped employees through the process of supplying the kind of feedback that drives stronger improvements than an annual review ever could.

Through this analysis, you will collect information about each employee's confidence in their colleagues' ability to execute. Many years of fine-tuning research from institutions such as Deloitte & Touche and engaging in discussions with change-management experts have informed my thinking about how to frame the questions for an effective organizational network analysis. While I will provide you with sample questions later, here are some key characteristics that I've found produce productive responses, regardless of the questions specifically asked:

- *Keep it positive.* Instead of asking if someone has concerns about a colleague, focus on what others do well and how they might improve.
- *Focus on the future.* The past is only there to learn from. The question now is, *What can the future look like?*
- *Avoid judgment.* I learned this one the hard way. I initially asked tribe members about performance satisfaction, which focuses on the past. It implicitly directs an employee to judge a coworker's actions,

placing the focus on the wrong thing and wrong person. Instead, focus on levels of confidence in future performance and how that might be improved. This places the emphasis on the feelings of the person answering the question about what the future looks like.

Getting good data requires trust. People will initially distrust the bot and how the data will be used. I regularly encounter conspiracy-minded employees who are convinced that I will use the data for some nefarious plan. No matter how much I try to reassure them, they see this as merely another example of bad corporate behavior. When I first met these types, I mentally discounted them. Later I realized that they had been institutionalized into that way of thinking by *bad corporate behavior*, and that it was my job to try to undo that damage. Later in the book, I recommend warming up with a "quantitative" analysis that begins laying the foundation for trust and empathy.

COACHING

Think about the best manager you ever had. They were experienced and used that experience to help you level up. They were always looking for opportunities for you to shine. They were patient and able to help you understand the problem that needed solving, and then ensured that you had the resources necessary to solve it quickly. They didn't assign you tasks but, rather, problems to be solved. They were proud of you when you came up with a solution better than the one they had proposed. They cheered your team on from the sidelines. They believed in surrounding themselves with people smarter than them, and that included you.

Guess what? They weren't operating as a manager; they were operating as a coach. Think about what sports coaches do. They help players hone their craft, teach them everything they know, and cheer them on from the sidelines. The same is true for a high-performance team. When the whistle blows, the team needs to be empowered to make a play based on the ground conditions they see in the moment. Can you imagine if football or baseball teams were run like we run companies?

"Tom Brady is ready to throw the ball, but the only person open is a fullback. He decides to send an email to the coach asking what he should do because there are no qualified running backs who could make the catch."

Adaptive teams are more akin to bionically augmented sports teams than to machines. Their members are fluid and understand how to take advantage of one another's strengths and weaknesses. Quarter after quarter, they help each other level up to be a better team member. Each member has a coach from elsewhere in the company to hold them accountable for acquiring new skills and making improvements.

HIRING AND FIRING

Most companies have an extraordinarily well-thought-out hiring process. Interestingly, many of these same companies don't have any sort of process for firing. It is as if a pattern of magical thinking has developed around firing. This thinking is, indeed, magical, since most companies have an attrition rate between 8 and 15 percent. It probably goes without saying that whether you are following the mechanical business philosophy or Adaptive, the lack of a termination process is not a best practice.

In a mechanical business, managers are responsible for firing. Sometimes employees make it easy to fire them by doing something that warrants immediate termination. Outside of that, most managers are slow to pull the trigger for the very human reason that it's incredibly uncomfortable to fire people. It's also very difficult to remove knowledge about an employee's personal life from the equation. Everyone knows Harry should be fired, but he is a single parent with three kids to support. As a human being, it's hard to overlook the circumstances of Harry's life, even if you also know that he is detrimental to the performance and health of your company. I don't know about you, but I don't know a single person who enjoys firing others.

Firing should be a process that is just as well defined as hiring and as transparent as possible. The rules and data must be readily available. As part of that data, employees should be able to see their *own* information, so they have a good grasp on where they stand at any given point in time.

This is where the coaching bot in Adaptive really saves the day. Quarterly 360-degree feedback gives employees a lot of lead time to make course corrections before it is too late. It also creates a wealth of documentation that supports any decision to terminate an employee. This is opposed to traditional termination processes that begin with an extensive documentation effort *after* a manager has decided to terminate someone's employment.

In my experience, people who have access to their own feedback data and can see that their termination is imminent will often leave the organization before they are fired. In companies where I have rolled out this type of system, the attrition rate has sunk to between 3 and 5 percent for good attrition (employees who elect to leave) as well as bad attrition (terminations). Also, understand that attrition isn't a dirty word; every company wants *some* attrition because it brings in new blood, which is necessary for a healthy company. It's also important to expunge people who are not a fit for the company, because those individuals can drive away or handicap the stronger performers.

A practice I've found to be empowering for everyone is to just put *everyone* on a performance improvement plans (PIP) right from the beginning! Shouldn't everyone be on a program to up their performance and not just the people who are at risk for termination? Shouldn't you be collecting documentation on every employee's performance all the time to find ways to help them level up so they can better serve the strategy? With this new way of thinking, nobody is treated differently. Everyone is prone to the same analyses—the only difference is the decisions made with the data collected.

Historically, this approach would have been logistically difficult to pull off. Terminating someone's employment is often far more difficult than hiring them in the first place. As you may have guessed, this is where bots can come to the rescue again. The important thing is changing the company culture to reset expectations that everyone is now on a performance and everyone needs to listen to their colleagues on how to improve to better serve the team and the strategy.

CHAPTER SIX

DATA ANALYSIS

While great leadership is somewhat of an art, there is a science to obtaining the information required to get a handle on what's *really* happening in your company to help you better lead. In this chapter, we'll discuss how to gather the important data that will help you optimally organize your network and grow individuals in ways that will serve both them and the company.

ORGANIZATIONAL NETWORK ANALYSIS

The information you obtain from the 360-degree feedback process I mentioned earlier can help you understand who the *real* power brokers are in your company. It will give you an overview of how people are connected—and disconnected—so that you can build your network around what's already working or correct what is not. Organizational network analysis is critical because every other decision you make will flow from the information gathered through these questions.

Once you have this 360-feedback in hand, you can understand what your team really looks like—how individuals' function within it, how the team works, and what their relationships look like. You will be shocked at how obvious your team's strengths and weaknesses are. The weaknesses will be so clear that they cannot be ignored.

Organizational network analyses will also highlight the cohesion, or lack thereof, of every group within your company. They show how interconnected all the individuals on a team are. Graphed out, a well-structured team will look like there are a lot of lines going all over the place. This shows that there are frequent interactions and collaborations among team members.

Cytoscape, a popular open-source graph-visualization tool, is an excellent way to visualize organizational network analyses. It is remarkably easy to use, can accommodate thousands of nodes and relationships, and produces visually stunning graphs. The tool enables you to slice and dice the results so that you can quickly find surgical changes to improve the health of the entire network.

ORGANIZATIONAL NETWORK ANALYSIS IN PRACTICE

Incorporating an organizational network analysis into your business will allow you to see the cohesion of your network and your team. Collaboration technologies and bots are perfect for this application. Are people well connected? Are they overly connected? Or are they not connected at all? This process should be repeated quarterly. The frequency of this process is another reason why it's helpful to complete the process through bots in your collaboration platform.

It is amazing what the data can reveal. Often, I have discovered that one person has ten lines coming into them. That is usually the same person who is always complaining that they are too busy to get their own job done. Of course, they are! So many people are relying on them; they need some relief or reorganization. Alternatively, you may find members who are very poorly connected to the rest of the network. Some might even have just a single incoming link. Why are they here again?

In a hierarchy, the disconnect between what is and what is perceived to be is the root of disengagement. The manager with underserved positional power, the capable employee who has never been promoted, the employee who gets inexplicably promoted, etc. If you plan to maintain a hierarchical business model, you will want to realign the hierarchy with what you actually see in the network to create a higher degree of integrity. Remember that in business, titles are the currency of recognition, so you can create more engagement by aligning people's contributions with their title. Since this feedback is being sourced through employees, they already *know* who is effectively running the show. You are simply identifying a disconnect between what's on paper and what exists in reality. In a hybrid or mature Adaptive model, the goal is to achieve balance through this information. People should have a reasonable number of connections coming into them (reasonable generally falls somewhere in the five through seven range). You may have to move things around to achieve this.

The information collected allows you to see which parts of your organization are not gelling and which are tightly knit. It will allow you to draw clear correlations between relationships and business results. It will clearly point to the areas of your company or team that are disconnected, disjointed, or misaligned. While it is sometimes shocking to see this information on paper, most people aren't all that surprised by the results. On some level, you've suspected these dynamics all along.

During a discussion about the importance of terminating poor performers, I once heard an executive say, "Look, we all know who the poor-performing employees are. Just do the right thing and remove them from the organization." He is right. Chances are that on some level you already know who is working and who is not. The beauty of the organizational network analysis is that it provides objective data that makes all this starkly apparent, with documentation to back up your decisions.

The question now is what to do with this information.

When you begin analyzing your business, you will find that there is a lot of dead wood. I have yet to roll this out to a new team and not immediately see that somewhere between 10 percent and 30 percent of the organization is sparsely connected and underperforming. You will realize there are people who aren't effective, people whom no one likes, and others who seem to be disconnected from the network completely (they receive no feedback). This requires pruning action.

You will also notice people who are in the wrong place in the network; by simply moving them, you will get a productivity boost. While your attrition rate will decrease over time in an Adaptive organization, it might rise initially as you name people who do not naturally fit into the network.

A key part to this process is coaching, which we will cover in detail. By moving toward an Adaptive organization, you will use the feedback at your disposal to create a coaching plan that holds employees accountable for bettering their performance in the coming quarter to better execute against the strategy. If they cannot get their performance up to acceptable levels with this kind of support, they are either on the wrong team or in the wrong company.

While this is not always a pleasant process, rest assured that the people whose employment you end up terminating were slowing down the tribe, whether you were actively aware of it or not. Furthermore, they were unhappy, knowing that their situation was suboptimal. Now you have the data to understand what's happening and can help them decide what's right for both the employee and the team.

In the six years I have been running the Adaptive Experiment, not one termination ended up hurting the team. Invariably, everyone was better off, able to work more efficiently and effectively. The first time I had to terminate someone I truly liked, I was concerned the decision would harm the team. Had I been in a traditional management role and not had all the data at my disposal, I would have told everyone to suck it up and continued to employ the struggling team member. However, the wisdom of the crowd turned out to be right. We were all better off.

Michael Arena, who applied network organizational techniques at GM, authored a terrific book on how to think about optimizing social networks called *Adaptive Space: How GM and Other Companies Are Positively Disrupting Themselves and Transforming into Agile Organizations*. I encourage you to check out his work for a broader treatment of how to optimize networks. He did not consider the effect of collaboration platforms and bots, but the optimization principles he covers are the same. Below in chapter 7 on coaching, I'll cover network adjustments that I found during the Adaptive Experiment.

THE EVOLUTION OF ORGANIZATIONAL NETWORK ANALYSIS

As helpful and informative as organizational network analyses can be, they are often far more reliable over time than in the initial round. As I wrote above, the first round of 360 feedback is usually not helpful. Mistrust, cautiousness, and fear of retribution will jade the feedback, making it barely useful.

In most cases this mistrust is warranted. Most employees have reason to worry that, despite what they are being told, the goal of this data is for something that's not to their benefit, such as a layoff or reorganization. From an employee's point of view, moving into a flatter, fluid model can be unnerving because it does not give them a place to hide, which hierarchies do. In a hierarchy, an individual's role is buried under a manager. Moving into this new model rips that cover off so that everyone is more clearly visible. Of course, this is a good thing for those people who want a voice and an active role on the team.

In weak teams, a small ratio of strong players is often carrying most of the water. For such employees, the first organizational network analysis can be wildly exciting. They can *finally* demonstrate their own skill and identify all the problem areas on the team. Of course, the remaining team members are terrified because they have been hiding out and are about to be unmasked.

I remember a colleague who said, "I wouldn't survive a quarter in that model." He was right. Although this person was a high-ranking manager, his direct reports did not like or respect him, and he knew they would oust him in a heartbeat. Imagine being this person, knowing this, and then laughing it off. Remind me not to work for that guy.

As discussed earlier, Google has done some interesting research that points to the fact that psychological safety is the critical element of high-performance teams. Psychological safety is built on trust that your company is going to use the data you are supplying to make things better. Even after launching the quantitative analysis, the first round of 360 analyses will show only broad-brush strokes.

It will point most accurately toward obvious problems. Use this information to make just a few modifications in these obvious cases. This proves to the organization that you are willing to take steps to make things better for them. It also proves that you are *listening* to what your employees are telling you. In other words, with these surveys, you are taking steps toward becoming a servant leader.

Depending upon your company culture, you may be able to establish trust after taking small and obvious actions on this first round of surveys. If your culture is more broken, it may take three rounds before employees buy into the fact that these surveys are working to their benefit, that you are listening and acting based on their experience.

To get around this, I recommend using bots to perform a quantitative analysis first. Instead of asking 360 questions about a colleague's performance, instead merely ask *who* they are working with and perhaps a few objective facts about that relationship. We will cover what that looks like shortly.

The point is that before you can trust your team to be honest and forthcoming in their feedback, you must first earn the trust of your team. If you have been working as a hierarchical company, employees may very well be suspicious of the true motives behind this analysis. No matter what reasons you give them for taking this step, there is likely to be mistrust.

A WARM-UP EXERCISE—A QUANTITATIVE ANALYSIS

The first step to using organizational network analyses to get periodic, high-quality feedback is to start building trust. If you don't have a bot to do the work, then start with a simple survey that merely asks for objective facts. A survey can result in messy data, but it will still yield incredible insights. There are tools out there that can help you achieve the same effect with higher-integrity data. Of course, this is where chatbots really shine because they can reach out to everyone in the organization on an individual basis to work with them to collect this data. Regardless of the mechanism, consider asking each employee these three simple questions:

- Whom do you work with to get stuff done?
- How often do you work with them (hourly, daily, weekly)?
- What is the priority of the relationship relative to your work?

These questions are easily answered without any emotional or political fireworks. Just the facts, ma'am. The answers will enable you to rapidly map out how work gets done independent of the org chart. It will also enable you to ferret out implied positional power.

With the collected data in hand, you can now quickly begin making surgical changes to improve collaboration.

TIME TO BUILD TRUST—DO SOMETHING

Once you have acquired this information, you will quickly see the true power holders, key-person risks, and duds. Now it's time to take some action in response to the data you've collected. This will prove to the company that you are serious about making changes to become a flatter, more fluid company that is serious about scaling empathy and trust.

This might involve transitioning team members to different areas of the company. Maybe you find someone who is totally overburdened and could use some help. Maybe you find someone who is disconnected from the team and needs to be better integrated. It might involve shaking up management. What's important is that you make modifications based on the information you gathered. This shows you mean business. You are not only asking your team members for feedback; you are also listening to what they are telling you. You are willing to do something that makes their working lives better.

Hierarchical organizations typically do not make decisions based on broad-based input. They make decisions based on appointed power and theories about how things "should" work. On the contrary, the Adaptive approach analyzes how work *actually* gets done and makes changes based on empirical data. Taking a step in this direction will begin to establish—or strengthen—trust with your employees. They will see that you are listening to what they have to say and taking action based on that.

Once you have reached this point of the Adaptive model, you have transitioned into the role of servant leader. Even if your title has not changed, your position and relationship with your employees has. You are looking at how work is getting done independent of titles and then producing strategies to increase throughput in service to feedback from employees.

360 FEEDBACK

While the quantitative organization network analysis focuses on facts and the working relationships within the organization, 360 feedback, which can be bot or survey driven, seeks the opinions of team members about how their colleagues can improve. This will enable individuals to push forward with shared strategic objectives as a unit, checking and supporting one another, without the centralized command-and-control structure of a management chain.

With 360 feedback, you want to get to the heart of how effective a person is within their role, how knowledgeable they are about a subject area, and things they could do to improve. The scores will be used by the individual being evaluated and their coach to determine areas for growth and refinement, which we'll dive into in the next chapter.

Although 360 feedback focuses on questions about how to improve an individual's performance, that is not the only information collected. Over the years, I have found 360 feedback is most effective and revelatory when it is self-directed. This means that instead of telling Frank he must fill out a survey about Sarah, it is far more effective to tell Frank to provide feedback about whomever he benefitted from or impacted the most in the past quarter. If he doesn't provide feedback on Sarah, that is information too!

This is not how most organizations collect 360 feedback. Generally, this sort of survey is issued by another person when there is a known performance problem. I've had colleagues tell me that they have "been 360'd." In this version of a 360, anonymous bots fan out across the organization on a regular, predictable basis with the simple question, "Would you like to provide coaching feedback for anyone this quarter?"

This strategy simultaneously accomplishes two things. First, it allows employees to decide whom to evaluate, taking your company yet another step away from operating on positional power. Frank is not evaluating Sarah because you told him to; Frank is evaluating Sarah because she influenced him in some way and he is deciding to evaluate her. Second, approaching feedback from this self-directed point of view provides an ongoing look at how the relationships within your organization are functioning and shifting. Are the power holders remaining the same? Who is significantly contributing to the tribe? Where is the dead wood?

It is important to remember that a nonanswer is an answer. If someone on your team receives no feedback, this is valuable information. In fact, the absence of information about a team member is as valuable as the presence of information. Why is it that Sarah did not get any feedback? It's because, for one reason or another, everyone avoids Sarah. It is highly indicative that she is not an important part of the team, either because she's not pleasant to interact with or because she's not performing.

As with organizational network analysis, it will take awhile for 360 feedback to be reliable enough to drive significant action. However, training team members on how to provide effective feedback helps speed the efficacy of the process. (We will discuss what training should entail later in this chapter). This training process establishes transparency, which helps build trust. With this, the team is positioned for a clearer path to success and transformation.

Much like the first time you gather information in the organizational network analysis, the first 360 feedback will produce garbage to some extent. People don't trust the system yet, and their feedback reflects that distrust. Employees have no sense of what the person in a position of power is going to do in response to this feedback, and this creates an unnerving situation for employees.

If you request this initial 360 feedback in an effort to strengthen and connect a team, chances are it is because the team has a lot of negative energy. In some situations, the initial round of feedback might almost feel like a release for employees. Regardless of where on the spectrum the feedback falls—evasive or overly fiery—the fact remains that it is not useful or indicative of the true situation. Instead, you should think of the first round (or even the first few rounds) as a trial run.

Still, as was the case with your initial organizational network analysis feedback, you have to do something with this information in order to show that you are serious about it. This will help establish trust so that later rounds *are* informative and useful. Deep trust is just as inherent to a tribal atmosphere as mistrust is to a hierarchy. You have an opportunity at your fingertips to begin instilling that. Whatever action you take should not be scary; no one should be fired as a result. However, if two people who should be connected—and, thus, reviewing one another—are not, you can ask some questions about that. Acting on these questions is not okay, but opening a conversation is. In other words, you can use this initial data as the impetus to gather more data. You can use it to establish a sense of transparency among team members.

In my experience, it takes about three rounds of feedback before the information is reliable and indicative of what is happening in an organization. You should see an increasing amount of reliability with each round. The second round is usually of a slightly higher quality than the first. In this round, it is imperative that you act on feedback that improves the health of the network. This demonstrates that the information being obtained is important. For instance, if the feedback points to an ineffective team member, it is time to have a conversation with that team member to explain specifically how they need to improve.

Initially, feedback is often saccharine. This indicates that people don't yet trust the process. It's also because people are generally nice and want to be kind to one another.

However, as employees become more accustomed to and

trusting of the process, feedback becomes more critical and hard-hitting. Team members come to understand that the feedback is being utilized as a tool for the growth of both the individual and the team. Critical feedback gives people something to work with. It gives them somewhere to grow, and it feeds the coaching program in ways that optimize the system.

During the execution of the Adaptive Experiment, I was also part of the experiment. Yes, this violates research protocols, but I felt it was important for me to experience the same processes as the other participants. It was also important for all the participants to know that I was not above the process; I was subject to it. Despite my station within the team as the reporting manager, I received a lot of hard-hitting feedback. I grew more over that six-year period than at any other point in my career. I wasn't the only one who felt this way. After I shut the experiment down in January 2019 to start a company around these ideas, many of the participants reached out to tell me how much they had grown while working in the Adaptive model.

Once you have established your 360-feedback program, it is helpful to introduce it to employees as early as the job interview phase. Obviously, the questions for candidates will not be exactly the same as they are on the employee survey, but they should be in alignment and drive at skills, productivity, and reliability, all of which are characteristics of high-performing teams. This will provide candidates with a good feel for your culture and its expectations in practice. It will also help you understand if a candidate is a good fit.

The coaching team should analyze the 360-feedback survey questions once a year to ensure they are delivering the desired results. Typically, only minor tweaks are necessary. Even minor changes should not be made more frequently than yearly because you must work off a stable standard for the year to see meaningful trends. Changing the questions will disrupt your data. This data must be reliable because you will use it to make key financial and termination decisions.

The feedback must be open and transparent so employees can see where they are excelling and where they need to improve. We will discuss how this feedback is used for measurable growth in the next chapter.

360-FEEDBACK SURVEY QUESTIONS

Ask no more than six questions on your 360-feedback survey to keep the process from being overly onerous. An overly complex or time-consuming survey will negatively impact the information you receive and the number of coworkers that employees are willing to review. For long surveys, the last questions are throwaway.

Over the six years of the Adaptive Experiment, I refined these questions to find the most useful qualities in individual team members to build a strong network. These were my team values, though they may not be your team values. Experience and research have informed these questions, including that of Deloitte & Touche, which has compiled a lot of valuable information about what creates a highly collaborative team.

I have found that the team values yield the greatest amount of actionable feedback for increasing team cohesion. The first four values will be accompanied with a scoring range of one to ten. They cover IQ issues and drive an individual's performance scores that will be used for pay adjustments and termination. The last two values are diagnostic in nature, based on EQ, and will not be included in an individual's performance scores.

Over the years, I have had a lot of questions over that very last statement—why not include someone's EQ scores in their overall performance score? Simply put, the EQ questions tend to serve as an escape valve for pent-up negative energy. Someone may be loath to give low marks to a jerk who is also a strong performer. But if you give them a way to express their displeasure that will not impact someone's pay or employment with the company, that is often where you get the most clarifying data. Furthermore, it is easier to make organizational decisions based on IQ data because it tends to be less subjective (note that I didn't say that IQ data is objective).

IQ Values

These first four values will be scored on a scale of one through ten, driving the individual's performance scores.

Each question about the team values should be framed in the form of "How well did this person do last quarter?" Then ask for feedback on what they could do to improve performance in the coming quarter.

Reliability

How reliable was John Doe in the previous quarter?

How would you suggest he improve?

To create a tribal culture, colleagues need to know that they have one another's backs and that team members will follow through on their commitments 100 percent of the time. Sometimes people score low on reliability because they are not reliable, but often this score, when combined with the organizational network analysis, spotlights imbalances on the team that could be driving individuals to be unreliable.

Case in point: I worked with a guy named Kevin who would put Gandhi and Mother Teresa to shame. He was quite literally one of the nicest people I have ever met. Kevin was universally loved. However, his feedback showed that, nice as he was, Kevin didn't move very fast and people considered him unreliable. Combined with the organizational network analysis, we came to realize that Kevin was like a pincushion. He was so nice that *everyone* came to him, and Kevin couldn't say no to anyone. As a result, he couldn't move fast on one person's needs because he was moving as fast as he could on many people's needs and constantly scrambling to deal with unplanned work.

Everyone thought he was a slowpoke because they only saw their little sliver of his work. Kevin's low score on reliability pointed out an issue that we were able to resolve by coaching Kevin to say no. Very quickly, not only did Kevin's reliability score go up, but the rest of his scores did as well; he now has the bandwidth to do a great job on a smaller number of things, and people's perceptions of his reliability have changed.

Skill

How would you rank John Doe's skills in the last quarter?

What would you suggest he do to improve?

The company Valve refers to the T-shaped employee as someone who is good at what they do across the board but also has at least one deep well of expertise. This is what we want to cultivate—a team in which everyone has an area (or areas) of deep expertise that makes them valuable to the tribe. Different tribe members may cite different areas of expertise when surveying the same employee. This is good! Remember, we want tribes to be fluid and ever-evolving, acquiring new skills to help drive the company strategy. This means that while one person may consider an employee's area of expertise to be leadership, another may view it as their ability to develop great code.

"Skill" is a flexible term that might involve technical expertise, EQ, time management, or a range of other more nebulous skills that positively impact the team's results.

Case in point: A very green DevOps engineer joined our team at the recommendation of a colleague. He interviewed well, but everyone was leery because he had so little experience. He didn't have a college degree and had previously managed a Dairy Queen. "You will see" was our colleague's retort every time we expressed our concern. He was right, and this junior engineer quickly turned into a powerhouse.

Despite his impressive ascent, feedback about his skills highlighted that he still lacked the credentials that could round out his impressive potential. So, we tasked him with pursuing the most challenging AWS certifications he could find. We all rooted for him before each exam and cheered when he did well and supported him when he didn't. In the end, however, it worked. He eventually secured certifications that only one other person in the company held.

Productivity

How would you rate John Doe's productivity over the previous quarter?

What would you suggest he do to improve his productivity?

Even the most reliable and skilled team member is not going to add value to the team if they are not productive. The tribe exists to produce business value.

Being productive does not always—and I would even argue *rarely* does—look like working ten or fifteen hours a day. When you ask about productivity, you are looking for impact and results, not the time spent getting to that point.

Case in point: We had an incredibly talented team member who could write code that would make angels weep. Let's call him Drew. When Drew took our online coding exam, the resulting code made us all stop to behold its beauty. We couldn't wait for him to join our team and apply those incredible skills to our codebase.

After he joined, his skill-related scores were through the roof. Everyone was learning from him, and he helped us implement several critical practices. He was also slow. Incredibly slow. Painfully slow. This despite working long, hard days. As a result, his productivity scores were in the toilet, wrecking his overall scores.

His challenge was that he overthought every line of code. He also had a background in security, which tends to addle one's brains, causing him to see shadows everywhere.

We eventually realized that he should not work on our most sensitive systems. The stress of working on that code was killing his productivity. However, the value he brought the team in the form of code reviews, best practices, and the like was incredibly valuable. So, we guided him toward less critical systems that helped the entire team and gave him a place to continue contributing to the entire group, which happens to be the next topic we will discuss.

Contribution

How would you rate John Doe's contribution over the previous quarter?

What would you suggest he do to improve his contribution?

Of all the questions we have looked at so far, contribution can be the most nebulous to define. Contributing to the team and producing are not always the same thing. For example, Tammy might be on the hook to write a python code for the team. That is what she is producing as an individual. However, if in the course of writing that code she creates a new process or tool to help the team in a more general way, that is a durable contribution to the tribe. Tammy has now contributed to her network's strength in a way that will survive after she leaves. That is important!

With this question, we are looking for people who make a durable contribution to the team's strength that will last beyond their time with the team.

Let's return to Drew from the case study above. One of the most powerful practices Drew put in place was a code review process. I remember when he first proposed this, and the team decided to adopt it. There was howling. There was gnashing of teeth. There was rending of clothes. There were cries of "This is slowing us down and killing our productivity!" I was, to say the least, a bit anxious about what would happen next. Drew amplified this reaction through his code reviews, which were fierce and unrelenting.

Then, after a few months of this, we hit smooth air. People began chicken-sexing good code because they had Drew looking over their shoulder saying, "Good code" and "Bad code." In the end, the code review process he implemented was one of the most influential things we did for our effectiveness as a team.

Drew eventually left, but his contribution became part of the team's legacy value.

EQ Questions

The following EQ values are designed to diagnose issues that can potentially be alleviated through coaching. What do you do with someone who gets great marks on the IQ team values but low marks on EQ team values? You try to coach them. What if they get great EQ scores but low IQ scores? You help them move to a more productive spot within the company or move them out of the company.

As mentioned earlier, this is also an area of the survey that allows respondents to vent when necessary. If someone has been a jerk over the past quarter, team members can let out their frustration without damaging their coworker's overall score. It is important to provide a release valve so that negative perceptions about an employee don't pollute scoring questions. It also gives individuals an opportunity to learn about the issues others have with them so they can be remediated through coaching.

Energy

How much positive energy do you get from this person?

What would you suggest to them to improve that in the coming quarter?

In his book *Creativity, Inc.: Overcoming the Unseen Forces That Stand in the Way of True Inspiration*, Pixar CEO Ed Catmull writes about "the spirit in the room" as a critical team value necessary for high-performing teams. In his book *The No Asshole Rule: Building a Civilized Workplace and Surviving One*, Stanford University professor Robert I. Sutton explains how jerks are not worth hiring or keeping employed.

So, with this team value, we want to get to the root of how a person affects the team from an energetic standpoint.

Are they additive or detrimental? How much positive energy do they generate for the team?

Case in point: We had a wildly talented engineer who had built a technology that we decided to create an entire product and team around. Let's call him Paul. He was insanely smart and checked all the boxes on his IQ values. He was reliable to a fault. His skills were above everyone else on the team. He was insanely productive. Finally, his contributions to his team became the foundation of how they defined themselves.

He was also an insufferable jerk. He tended to argue endlessly about proposed solutions and was incredibly suspicious about his team members' intent. Consequently, his energy scores were abysmal. These poor energy scores ended up being a leading indicator of faltering performance.

Because he was so hard to work with, he became increasingly isolated. This then resulted in deteriorating scores. Meanwhile, another engineer with solid, but not legendary skills had quietly grown their sphere of influence, which made matters even worse for Paul. The key difference? This individual was a total sweetheart whom everyone loved working with.

Perceived Improvement

How much has this person improved over the previous quarter?

What would you suggest to them to improve even more?

This team value is separate from the mathematical improvements an employee demonstrates in their scores. Instead, we are driving at the experience individual colleagues are having with their improvement. What perception do people have of a team member's performance improvement?

Often, the answers to this question can be flat. You will see answers like, "Mary is just as awesome as she's always been," or "Ted is the same as usual." That is great if Ted is great and just as telling if Ted is not! However, sometimes you also might receive feedback that an employee has slipped over the past quarter. This is not grounds for termination, but it does provide valuable diagnostic material.

TRAINING EMPLOYEES TO GIVE GOOD FEEDBACK

Before issuing the 360-feedback survey on team values, sit down with your team and explain what the questions mean, what you're really trying to get at through them, and why you're doing this in the first place. Let employees know that the purpose of this feedback is to create a highly collaborative, agile team that can manage itself and improve as a group.

Over the course of the Adaptive Experiment, I collected a wealth of feedback. I was able to perform a natural language analysis on all that feedback to tease out features in the feedback that appeared to be correlated with stronger improvement over time.

What I found was that subjective, positive, and actionable features are the keys to productive feedback. Of those three, subjective feedback was the most surprising. Subjective feedback contains opinions and feelings. I found this utterly confounding. When I mentioned this with the test subjects, the response was eye-opening. If you are working on a highly collaborative, flat, fluid team, relationships matter. Knowing what your peers think about you matters.

This flies in the face of the mechanical business philosophy that tells us to "not take it personally, it is just business." Managers are taught to focus on the facts, despite the reality that most of those "facts" are subjective managerial observations. If our goal is to strengthen collaboration, we must recognize that *it is personal*.

I'm sure your own experience points to the fact that even the most highly skilled person will impede a team if they are mean-spirited or arrogant. One of the goals of these surveys is to help coworkers understand how their performance is impacting the team on a personal level. Do they make the team feel good? Do they help create a sense of cohesion and trust? Many people are unaware of how their behavior impacts others. Providing this type of illuminating feedback can completely alter both individual performance and the strength of the team.

With this, it is also important to clarify that subjective opinion need not be negative. In fact, you want to encourage people to stay as positive as possible, while remaining honest and effective. In teams that have been plagued with animosity for years, it can be easy to blast coworkers. Subjective positive feedback tends to yield bigger personal improvements over time. This does not mean that survey respondents should provide false or dishonest feedback. Even negative feedback can be reframed in a positive way. Feedback should also be actionable. What does this person need to do to level up their performance in the eyes of their peers?

As part of the training process, it is also important to advise team members that they don't have to rate everyone. Instead, they want to concentrate on the people who come to mind, whether it is because they were helpful or because they hindered an individual or the team over the past quarter. Rating people with whom you have little interaction, or only slight knowledge of, is not helpful because it does not result in high-integrity feedback. In other words, if you work with Bob once a month, you are not going to have the best gauge of his performance on a day-to-day basis. He is not the person you should be prioritizing for feedback.

If you choose to roll out these surveys through a bot, the bot can review the feedback in real time and provide live coaching on how to improve their language. As part of my research, I counted up the number of attempts it took for my colleagues to provide effective feedback as determined by the bot. Over time, the number of attempts went down and the quality of the feedback went up. In other words, the bots interactively taught people how to write good feedback, and those lessons stuck from one quarter to the next. The bots were helping people chicken-sex good feedback!

I saw a change in the one-on-one interactions in the team over time as well. Some people ended up using the bot for target practice—telling the bot what they thought in raw, visceral terms and then letting the bot instruct them on how to do better. This back-and-forth between the person and the bot enables them to prepare for face-to-face interactions later. One person on the team told me they would write their review three times, using the first two attempts to serve as a way to just blow off steam.

LOOKING AT SCORING

Once the team trusts that the data collected will drive a process of continuous improvement in service of the strategy, you can use that data to drive merit increases, coaching assignments, and termination. Once you are to a place where you can use the data to make these kinds of decisions, you have achieved an immense accomplishment.

By driving compensation and termination from scoring based on crowdsourced data, it removes the last vestige of positional power from the team. Instead of team members focusing on making their boss happy, they instead focus on all of their colleagues' ability to effectively collaborate with one another to drive the strategy.

MERIT INCREASES

If you decide to use merit increases and not pay-for-performance, you can use the average of the IQ team values as a foundation. You can get sophisticated with this data to create a clear system for determining wage increases. As we discussed, I like to incorporate a transparent model that allows everyone to plug in their scores to predict salary increases. Say you have a team of twenty and can only afford to increase salaries by 4 percent across the entire group. You can provide a graph or spreadsheet to demonstrate to employees how their scores will align with the percentage of increase. For example, employees scoring between ninety-five and one hundred could receive a 4 percent increase, whereas those in the ninety through ninety-four range could receive 3 percent, and so on.

The important thing about a system like this is that it does away with unpredictability, politics, and capricious processes. In a more traditional system, Harriet's manager might tell her, "Our financials weren't good this year, so you're only getting a 2 percent raise." Meanwhile, Rob's manager tells him, "Hey! You did a fantastic job this year—here is a 5 percent increase."

HIGH SCORES

With a scoring range of, say, one to ten, it seems intuitive that we want employees to score as close to ten as possible. This is not the case. We want strong scores, but scores close to ten indicate either that employees are not putting energy into insightful, critical feedback or that it's time for your perpetual high scorers to stretch themselves, take on new challenges, and grow.

A woman I worked with named Amy is a good example of that latter scenario. Amy is good at what she does and always gets great scores. She is great at self-regulating and will often let me know she's bored and wants to do something else. I encourage this, but warn that her scores might initially tank as she learns a new function. Her response is always the same: "I'm fine with that." She is willing to risk exchanging merit increases for new opportunities.

It's best to let employees like Amy spread their wings and go somewhere else in the company. Perhaps they can start coaching others. Perhaps they can strengthen another part of the company. Whatever the outcome, it's better that she stays in the network than goes to work for a different company.

Although Amy's scores initially tank, by the second quarter, they are back up. Adaptive ensures that she is rewarded for demonstrating new skills, as opposed to being penalized because her scores initially take a hit. We understand what her scores mean and provide Amy with the support she needs to grow and expand. She has the bandwidth to move from one network to another within the company and isn't unfairly penalized in terms of merit increases—despite the fact that her scores dip and rise.

On the other hand, there are the Vinnys of the world. Vinny consistently gets great scores. He's amazing at what he does. The problem with Vinny is that he gets stuck on one thing and becomes a key-person risk. This happens with him on a regular basis, so we are constantly telling him that he must contemplate what he wants to do next, move on, and find another opportunity to pursue. In short, Vinny needs to work on his collaboration skills.

This causes Vinny considerable angst. He initially perceived our desire to tackle his key-person risk as a slight, but then he realized we were looking out for his best interests, as well as the best interests of the team and tribe. When Vinny stayed in one place for too long and created key-person issues, he actually hurt the tribe.

Vinny is not alone. Most people—particularly those who have been ensconced in a hierarchy—seek stasis or find themselves in stasis. They like to do one or two things well and be good in their part of the network. Change unnerves them and stasis provides a sense of safety. However, this sense of safety is artificial; outside forces are acting on us at great rates and with significant force.

STABLE SCORES

Another thing to watch out for is statistical variance from quarter to quarter. Individuals with high variance in their scores are bouncing up and down in their performance. You never know what you are going to get. Let's look at Amy again. Remember that she likes to move on after she has mastered something because she gets bored. Her variance is naturally going to be higher, so we can work with her to blunt that effect before she joins a new team. This might include up-front training or interning with a team to familiarize herself with their content.

John is another example of fluctuating scores. John is smart but a terrible team member. Some quarters his scores are fantastic because he delivers on a piece of hard-hitting research and everyone is impressed. But when his colleagues put John's research into production, it turns into a hot mess and everyone hates him. This shows that John's collaboration skills need work and that he needs to be coached on how to deliver solutions that are easier to put into production.

Scores with low statistical variance from quarter to quarter are another concern. These employees have good, solid scores and great relationships, so it makes sense to leave them be, right?

No. These people are easy to overlook because you want to focus on the low scorers. The problem with that is that the low scorers are probably going to be terminated from the team anyway. In the meantime, you have ignored the employees with good scores who may want to spread their wings, learn more, and grow. These employees deserve as much if not more of your attention as your low scorers.

LOW SCORES

As your feedback and the system become more reliable, you can more easily focus your attention on good employees by quickly weeding out the bad ones. You can't be a responsible steward for your company while just looking at terrible (or great) scores and not reacting in some way.

I advocate a policy in which an employee who scores below eight has ninety days to bring the score up before being terminated. I came to this policy in partnership with my HR partners. The approach dovetails with most termination processes. The key difference is that everyone is on an improvement plan all the time and the process generates lots of documentation along the way.

Ideally, your company will reach a place of maturity in

this system where the low-end score is agreed upon by the team itself and based on some initial baseline. This number might shift over time as the network raises the bar. When I started the Adaptive Experiment, the lowest acceptable score was seven. When I concluded the experiment, one team was set at 8.5. This rising bar strengthens the team, encouraging low scorers to level up and high scorers to remain energized. It creates in a system some degree of churn, which allows the company to bring in new skills as needed. This kind of renewal is healthy for the team.

Setting that bar too high can create artificial pressure to give everyone high marks. The low-end score should give everyone room for honest feedback without the risk of termination (unless the team has low confidence in that person's abilities).

We used to give a person three quarters to improve, but now that the process has been in place for a while and the feedback is reliable, we make good decisions more quickly based on scores. This type of decisive action based on scoring comes with maturity. Most companies need a couple of years of gathering data to get to that point. Everyone in the company understands that we base actions on feedback, so they understand the implications of providing negative feedback. It is the team's way of saying, "Coach that person or fire them."

Human resource departments like this scoring system because HR likes consistency and documentation. As I've written above, everyone in the Adaptive model is on an improvement plan of some sort in response to their feedback and coaching plans. No one is singled out, and the rules are the same for everyone. The data proves why someone needs to be let go and shows that the employee knew what changes were needed to avoid termination. They had the opportunity to improve and chose not to or were unable to.

CHAPTER SEVEN

COACHING

We associate coaches with sports. Soccer, football, baseball, and cricket coaches focus their energy in two directions: on the team holistically and on the individuals. They see the team as an organism to strengthen so that it can compete against other organisms like it. While coaches, of course, also work with the individuals on the team, it is the combination of these individuals that yields results. The goal is to maximize fluidity by coaching individuals to self-driven employees able to rapidly jump into new, complex collaboration patterns to solve big problems quickly.

When we talk about professional coaching, we always think about that in terms of the individual. Sure, we have team events and offsites, but executive coaches are typically with an individual for some amount of time, helping them level up their game. Individuals receive more intensive coaching than teams.

I suspect the reason behind this mindset is that, historically, it has been difficult to understand a business team holistically. With sports, this is much easier. The positions are all standardized. The plays are often documented in a "playbook" and explained in terms of easily understood movements that can be quickly executed in a moment of intense pressure.

This kind of coaching simply is not available to business teams because the plays and positions are not as well defined and likely never will be. However, organizational analyses afford us our first real opportunity to coach the business organism and the cell, the team and the individual. In this chapter, we will explore what it means to coach an Adaptive organization holistically.

THE POWER OF COACHING

Coaching represents a significant step in establishing an Adaptive model because it is an active, ongoing system that fights the institutionalization that most of us have experienced over the years. Coaching provides employees with a safe, predictable system through which they can cease abdicating self-determination to their manager and instead focus on the skills necessary to drive the company strategy and achieve deep, personal career satisfaction.

From this point, you can start looking at your team holistically because coaches will come to understand team members in a way that managers never will: as a complex web, not just a triangle in an org chart. With the combination of coaching and organizational network analysis, you can start treating the relationships among the individuals in your company as first-class entities. This represents a huge step forward for the company, because strong, collaborative relationships are a critical aspect of high performance. While coaching often concentrates on the individual, it can also be focused on enriching beneficial *relationships* that can enhance strategy execution.

Coaching will also allow you to get to the root of problems, which are often not what they appear on the surface. For example, one of the employees I coached, whom we'll call Luke, was highly rated on IQ but struggled with EQ. Luke had struggled before joining the Adaptive Experiment. Before joining us, he had been removed as the head of a functional department and was put on notice that if he did not clean up his act, he would be fired. The company had hired an executive coach for Luke, but that did not yield the change necessary. Things were looking bleak, and he was devastated and confused.

Luke was a likable person who was imminently qualified. He knew the business better than anyone else. His analytical mind could cut like a laser through the fog of the most arcane business and technology processes to unlock the problems within. Nobody could argue with him, and so they did not. Consequently, he was wearing blinders.

Luke had no idea what had gone wrong. He was a high-level vice president executing plans given to him by members of the executive team. As far as he could tell, he had executed on those plans perfectly. However, the functional area Luke had presided over ran him out on a rail. Before they terminated Luke's employment, one of the executives assigned him to the Adaptive Experiment to see what the effect might be.

In a traditional organization, I would have spoken with Luke's manager and a few peers and then formed my own opinion about how to proceed. This was how it transpired with the executive coach they hired for Luke, and that did not go anywhere. In the Adaptive model, however, we just put him to work and then waited for the feedback to come in.

In short order and with great feedback from his colleagues, we diagnosed the problem: Luke was an epically terrible listener. It would have been one thing for Luke to hear that from me, a relative stranger. It was something completely different for him to hear that from his colleagues.

Someone else on my team had already grappled with this issue and had improved their listening skills with the help of the book *Just Listen: Discover the Secret to Getting Through to Absolutely Anyone* by Mark Goulston. This is a terrific book that I recommend regularly, and so I recommended it to Luke, too.

What happened next is common for me in my coaching experience. Luke realized that his inability to listen effectively wasn't just impacting his professional life; it was impacting his personal life as well. After he finished the book, Luke told me that he had done tremendous damage to the relationship with his son. He realized how much work he had to do. Slowly, over the course of several quarters, Luke improved. In fact, he went on to become one of the best coaches on our team.

In my experience, this type of personal side effect is common.

Another example is a woman I coached whose colleagues felt she could be more productive in meetings. I recommended she consider reading *Crucial Conversations: Tools for Talking When Stakes Are High* by Kerry Patterson, Joseph Grenny, Ron McMillan, and Al Switzler. This is another classic that helps not only with listening skills, but also with the ability to navigate prickly conversations in a productive way. This book opened the woman's eyes in ways that surprised me. She saw a major dysfunction in her communication style that had impacted her relationships with friends and family. She eventually gave the book to her ex-husband and apologized for the mistakes she had made. She also shared it with friends. All of this translates to more productive employees because their professional and personal lives now afford them more time to be more effective.

In a more typical hierarchical situation, an employee like Luke may very well have been let go. He would have carried his inability to listen to his next job, and the damage would be repeated. In their book *What Got You Here Won't Get You There: How Successful People Become Even More Successful*, Marshall Goldsmith and Mark Reiter describe the many dysfunctions that blunt careers. This is one of my most reliable remedial coaching books. It seems like everyone has at least one of the dysfunctions listed, including me. I ended up working hard on at least three of the dysfunctions about which Marshall and Mark write, and my professional life is much better for it.

WHY COACHING?

As with a hierarchy, a flat and fluid organization can also get stale and fall into a rut over time. We can prevent this by stimulating one of the qualities most innate to human beings: their desire to grow, learn, and do new things. This is the basis of coaching and the reason coaching is the most essential part of an effective network organization. Without actively promoting and encouraging employees to evolve, they can stagnate. When individuals stagnate, so does the entire tribe. Coaching encourages improvement and rejuvenation in a way that paves the road for everyone to win.

When I first launched the Adaptive Experiment, I did not see the importance of a robust coaching program with a stable of trained, qualified coaches. Instead, I individually reviewed the feedback for everyone on my team, talked with everyone about what they might do to improve next time, and left it at that. This made me a great manager, but it did not create an Adaptive team. I was still in a position of power, and this method was stifling our transition to a highly effective team.

I modified the Adaptive model to replace the traditional manager role with a coach who was not necessarily me. Now, rather than having a manager direct how employees improve, we instead assigned a coach to each person. This coach focused on helping the employee grow, and nothing else. Not work assignments, not project work, just personal improvement in service of the company strategy.

Coaching improves business results because it helps each team member work to their maximum potential and toward the company's strategy without the corrosive effect of positional power. It is a highly effective long-term strategy and not the short-term tactical approach that managers shoot for by looking at work as piecemeal, one project at a time. Instead, we are growing employees and cultivating their skills so that their business results improve over the long run, thus improving strategy execution quarter after quarter.

Whereas employees in a hierarchy are expected to play the best role according to their title, employees in the Adaptive Experiment are expected to grow and advance so that they can better serve the company strategy in whatever way necessary. Their colleagues expect them to continuously enhance their influence, enabling them to have a bigger and bigger impact on the company, to take on new roles and more responsibility, and to do new things over time.

HOW COACHING WORKS

At the heart of coaching is the belief that people are trying their best. This means that coaching is *not* a vehicle for telling employees what to do. Remember, we are moving toward self-determination so they can operate autonomously to move the company strategy forward in whatever way they can. Coaching is also not about chastising or critiquing. It is about creating a path forward in the company for an individual that is plotted out based on the combination of data scores and an understanding of what the employee wants and needs, and how that relates to the company strategy. This is not a haphazard process; it is focused on individual needs triangulated with strategic objectives.

Coaching primarily serves two main functions in service to the company strategy: it resolves some of the network connection blips that show up on the organizational network analysis, and it provides a channel through which employees can grow outside of a traditional corporate ladder. The coaching staff will collaborate with one another to understand which skills are important to the company and share these skills with their team members. Coaching for effective employee growth will drive the natural evolution of a company with a focus on the strategy.

ALIGNING GROWTH AND STRATEGY

Use bots to orchestrate coaching aligned with the company strategy, and you are in an extraordinarily strong position indeed. If the strategy is not working, you can change it based on empirical market evidence. If the skills are not having the desired effect, you can challenge everyone to change them based on empirical evidence, too. The important takeaway is that we now have data we can use to make evidence-based decisions.

Coaching also helps redistribute and balance the connections within a network. A coach will work with those employees who have too many lines connecting to them, so that some of the energy directed toward them can be pointed elsewhere, effectively balancing the load of their relationships. On the flip side, coaches also try to figure out how to better connect those who are disconnected. I have never seen someone with a small number of connections receive a strong 360-feedback rating. In fact, it is always the opposite: a small number of connections and low scores go hand in hand. Increase a person's network, and typically not only do they benefit, but the team becomes stronger.

Working with an employee to critically evaluate their performance within the context of their feedback is often a transformative experience. This is particularly true when triangulated with the company strategy. Engagement surveys commonly find that employees are more engaged if they understand exactly how they are connected to the company strategy. Most companies fail miserably at this. There is often a massive gap between daily work and how that connects to the strategy. Designing your strategy with employee participation is critical. You strike coaching gold anytime you can identify an opportunity to tie together personal improvement and strategy execution.

Once the team member and coach have decided on a set of skills to emphasize, the coach will then do everything in their power to help the employee grow those skills. This involves setting aside time for growth and training in that area and creating a system of accountability through weekly coaching calls and the work-management system we discussed earlier. I call these "individual development objectives," the implication being that they are an extension of the strategic goals for the company.

This idea of accountability is inherent not only in coaching, but in the flat, fluid Adaptive model in general. The hierarchical model is missing accountability outside of the management team. In other words, at the end of the day it is your manager who will decide your worth to the company, not your colleagues. The team is responsible only for doing what the manager says—and the manager may very well not have all the knowledge necessary to understand how to best drive results. When things go poorly, this dynamic leads to employees saying, "I was just doing my job," and managers saying, "I had no idea they were doing that."

A critical element here is that it must be the coach who closes out the personal improvement objective, not the employee. In their book *Triggers: Creating Behavior That Lasts—Becoming the Person You Want to Be*, Marshall Goldsmith and Mark Reiter write about how having a human coach to hold you accountable for a personal change is absolutely critical. There is something about having a human accountability partner that drives results. This is where the sidewalk ends for bots, and humans still rule the roost, but bots can make sure that both parties are making progress toward closure.

ACKNOWLEDGING EMPLOYEE GROWTH

Coaches should work with the human resources department to develop a market-adjustment schedule for acquired, demonstrated skills. I credit my friend Lisa, an HR professional, for this critical addition to the Adaptive model. Previously, it was not clear how people would advance their careers and get the sugar rush that comes from a big pay increase. So that got us thinking: instead of paying more for a nebulous title, wouldn't it be better to pay for acquired skills in service to the company strategy? I referred to this idea earlier in the book as "pay-for-performance." This idea would have been harder to pull off in the days before the vast number of training websites hit the market. Nowadays, it almost seems irresponsible not to incorporate a strategy like this.

To implement a pay-for-performance model, work with HR to determine what the market value is for each strategic skill a team member can acquire. This is an inexact science, but it can keep you competitive in the labor market. You may also put some rules in place around how many people can pursue a skill. I also recommend using a third party to certify that someone has acquired a skill and can effectively demonstrate it.

Team members may have their own opinions about how they can become better employees and better execute the company strategy. Keep an open mind about employees' suggestions on areas for personal improvement. A coach's job is not to tell employees *how* to improve, but to help them improve in whatever way is important to them. Some personal improvements may just help an employee operate more effectively on the team. Even something like this can contribute to their merit increase. Other improvements can net a market adjustment. Amazing employees do both.

Usually, people must join another company to get a promotion. Now, we are rewarding people for their proven skillset, which incentivizes employees and keeps skills within the company. The amount of money they earn is no longer based on how well they interview and negotiate their salary but on how they actually perform and the skill they acquire and demonstrate.

I wonder if this is one of the reasons women are paid less than men. In a study titled "Do Women Avoid Salary Negotiations? Evidence from a Large-Scale Natural Field Experiment," Andreas Leibbrandt and John A. List note that women tend to avoid salary negotiations when there isn't an explicit approval to do so. In a later study titled "Research: Women Ask for Raises as Often as Men, but Are Less Likely to Get Them," Benjamin Artz, Amanda Goodall, and Andrew J. Oswald found that when women did ask for a raise they were often rebuffed. While starting salaries are outside the scope of this book, making use of market adjustments and the merit-increase model discussed earlier dramatically levels the playing field.

I've seen the impact of the pay-for-performance model triangulated with the strategy too many times to count. It didn't favor men or women. Instead, it favored go-getters regardless of gender. For example, I once had a young, inexperienced woman from India join the Adaptive Experiment on the recommendation of a friend who is the CEO of a large data analytics company. I was not prone to hiring "freshers," but my friend insisted that she was a go-getter unlike anything he had ever seen. Yet, this woman's salary was about 20 percent of her male counterparts. Gender dynamics in India warrant shelves of books, but in this case the discrepancy was egregious.

Step one was normalizing her salary based on a market assessment of her skills. Step two was coaching her on acquiring strategic skills, in her case AWS skills. She *crushed* it on skill acquisition. Each quarter was an exercise in keeping loaded up with ways to improve to better serve the strategy. Once the dust settled, this woman's salary nosed out a few of her male colleagues who had not been as insistent on skill acquisition for their individual development objectives.

Another problem with promotions is that they are usually based on an absence. Someone leaves the company and, as a result, another person is promoted. It is a lot like a monarchy, really. Look at poor Prince Charles, who has been waiting for decades to be king. At this rate, he may never be. Succession could skip right to Prince William should Prince Charles die before his mother. Within a company, there are a lot of princes and princesses cooling their heels, waiting for a turn that may never come in hierarchies.

There are no limitations when it comes to market adjustments other than your company's budget and strategic needs. Employees' progress and opportunity are not contingent upon someone else stepping down. Everyone in the company can constantly grow, improve, and be acknowledged without putting a cap on it.

Now, instead of a corporate ladder, we have something that looks more like a scouting badging system. For every badge an employee earns, the company figures out how much that badge would net the employee in the open market and increases their pay a commensurate amount. Another bonus to this system is that it alleviates competition. We are no longer functioning in a zero-sum game, where there is only one title to be bestowed upon a single employee. Everyone is not competing for the same thing. Instead, each employee is working on their own skillset, in a constant state of growth and acknowledgment.

Finally, with bots to help us with the paperwork, we will have a catalog of people who have acquired certain skills and won badges. If you need someone who has secured a skill, look no further than your friendly bot.

COACHING IN PRACTICE

You can set up different coaching teams for every department or network in your business. The size of these teams will depend upon the size of your company. I built bots to help this entire process. Each week the bot would reach out to ask for a quick update from everyone. The bot would then deliver this update to the coach. By facilitating this discussion, the bots helped make the endeavor more efficient.

With help from the bots, each live coaching session required that employees talk through their progress on individual development objectives with their coach. This enabled me to accommodate about eight objectives each week for a total of about two hours. Most of the people I coached had one or two objectives, enabling me to help five to eight people.

The coaching cycle will work in conjunction with the 360-feedback cycle, with employees selecting new objectives every quarter. Some research argues that a new pattern of behavior can be established in twenty-one days. The psychologist I've worked with on the Adaptive model believes that ninety days seems more reasonable. Quarterly iterations also fit well with the business cycle, since public companies post their earnings quarterly.

So whom do you choose to coach you on your objective? This is also where bots save the day. Bots can help this process by enabling individuals to choose someone to coach, to choose a coach, or even to put out a request for a coach. I can already hear you muttering at the page, "Who does this coaching?" Don't worry; I cover how to find your coach later in the book.

I also recommend that team members rotate coaches every quarter, unless there is a specific reason not to, such as working through goals that take two quarters to complete rather than one. Six months is as long as you want to stretch it, though. Without this rotation, it becomes all too easy to fall into a more traditional manager-direct report dynamic. An Adaptive organization that can accommodate strategic shifts must keep an eye out for anything that might pin someone down and cause organizational ossification.

Rotation is also important because it offers different

perspectives. One of the biggest weaknesses with the hierarchy is that you are putting your career growth in the hands of someone who brings exactly one perspective on how to be awesome—your manager. When it comes to medical advice, we are always encouraged to obtain a second opinion, but when it comes to career growth, we are told that our manager is the only person whose opinion matters.

Let's take a look at Sam, who had been working on a promotion to vice president. I happen to know Sam, and he is imminently qualified for this role. He leads a team that brings in more than 10 percent of the company's revenue and is a powerful servant leader. He was on the fast track to a promotion until his manager left for another company and his new manager had a completely different idea of what it meant to be a VP. Back to square one for Sam? Nope. Instead, he is now interviewing with other companies. A coaching scenario combined with a skill-acquisition program prevents situations—and losses—like this from occurring.

The logistics of what coaching entails will vary from one employee to the next, from one quarter to the next. Often, it involves training or learning. Other times, it involves working on more intangible skills. For example, I am a notorious workaholic. One quarter, an Indian yoga guru who also happened to work on my team suggested I try meditation to achieve better focus. I agreed to give it a shot, so he worked with me to incorporate different meditation techniques into my daily life. At a glance it might not be obvious that this drives my team closer to our business objectives, but in practice it does; it makes me healthier, more productive, and sets a better example for my team.

Other coaching agendas I've seen that have been highly effective have included exercise and weight loss. One woman I coached incorporated more exercise in her life, and each week she would post her fitness tracking data on her personal improvement objective. She lost twenty pounds. She used to be a nervous, occasionally snappy person who sometimes acted out in meetings. Today, she is so much happier and gives off much better energy. Her personal win was also a win for the entire team.

This holistic, whole-self focus points to another clear and key delineation between a traditional hierarchy and a network organization. Hierarchies are very task driven. Each employee's title indicates a static and set list of tasks they are expected to perform. However, that is only a small sliver of creating a healthy tribe. Team members who are not getting enough sleep or exercise or who are overworked or doing work they hate are going to be miserable, which damages the strength of the whole network. Coaching helps alleviate this.

Employees should provide feedback on the coaches and their coaching experience at the end of each quarter. This can be as simple as a rating on a scale of one to five accompanied with some brief feedback. Just as everything else in this system is dynamic, so is coaching. If a coach routinely receives low ratings, their assignments should be reconsidered, or that person should be removed from the coaching team.

Likewise, coaches should be given the opportunity to rate the person they coached on their progress and coachability. This all yields a tremendous amount of data that can enable companies to make good decisions based on empirical data.

CREATING BUSINESS GOALS FOR ALIGNMENT

We have talked a bit about how coaching aligns employee growth and a company's business results. One element that many companies miss when incorporating coaching and individual development objectives is that before either of these programs can be optimally executed, clear strategic objectives must be established. These objectives should serve as the north star for the company. Where do we want to go? What market do we want to capture? Where can we grow? And, most importantly, what skills do we need to foster in our company to get there? This last question is often missed, and it shouldn't be; it is imperative to align individual employees with the overall strategy to achieve the company's objectives.

Not only does building coaching and improvement plans around business goals create the best results; it also drives engagement. Highly collaborative network teams will crowdsource issues and problems. Clear business objectives give them a specific issue to rally around and engage with.

Clearly stated business goals are more important to an organization that is moving along the spectrum to become an Adaptive organization than they are for a traditional hierarchy. The hierarchy serves as a skeleton that keeps everything in the company static and in place. If a company is doing well and can afford to go on auto-pilot, no problem. The strategy is simple—do not mess with anything.

Increasingly, though, fewer and fewer companies can run on autopilot. It is difficult to think of a single industry that has not been disrupted by a recent technology or surprise international company coming in and disrupting the market. Company business objectives change all the time, even if that change simply involves drifting a little bit to the left or to the right. In situations like this, there is no time for constant reorganization. The solution is to instead hire great people who can understand the business objectives and reorient themselves to bring their skills to bear on the business problem that needs to be overcome.

INDIVIDUAL DEVELOPMENT OBJECTIVES

As an employee in a mechanical business, it is easy to fall into a rut. Every day you are exercising the same muscles. You are a cog in a machine always rotating in the same direction. It is no wonder, then, that when strategic change requires different muscles, nobody is ready. It is like asking an Olympic sprinter like Usain Bolt to play soccer. Just because you can run fast in one direction does not mean you can zigzag a soccer ball down a field. Yet we ask people to do this all the time.

To stay limber, everyone should be doing something to improve themselves or move a strategy closer to its desired outcome. If you are always stretching, you will not pull a muscle when told to break left. In hierarchical structures, performance improvement objectives are typically given to low performers as a red flag that they need to up their game or else. In an Adaptive coaching environment, *everyone* is given PIPs, regardless of their level of experience. While one goal is to level up those with low scores or room to improve, it's also important to utilize individual development objectives with high performers to better utilize their skills and allow them to share that sunshine with other team members. In this model, there is no differentiation between how high and low performers are treated. In each case, we are challenging employees to figure out how to stretch their skills and keep them engaged and invested in both their own performance and the performance of the company.

Each quarter, employees will work with their coaches to establish individual development objectives. The objectives will be based on a combination of business strategy and the review of the 360 feedback that has been provided by their colleagues. What skills will your company need to strategically cultivate moving forward? Individual development objectives serve as a way of aligning personal growth with business strategy.

Creating and working with individual development objectives takes away the opaque nature of promotions and pay raises, and provides clear evidence of how each individual needs to improve in order to perform more effectively in the eyes of their colleagues. The feedback they are receiving, whether positive or negative, is concrete. This feedback can now be parlayed into specific individual development objectives that individuals are on the hook to complete on a quarterly basis. At the end of each quarter, the employee will check in with their coach to confirm that these objectives either have been completed or are ongoing.

A critical component is that the coach must work with the employee to define criteria for proving they have, indeed, acquired the new skill. If this new skill is on the list of strategic skills that can net a market adjustment, then the bar is a little higher. For example, it is one thing to acquire an AWS certification and something else to demonstrate that you can use it.

This results in a transparent formula for calculating market adjustments. It serves as a way of ensuring not only that employees are constantly growing and improving, but that they are improving in response to what their colleagues see as areas for growth and refinement.

While market adjustments are great motivation for driving employee performance improvement objectives, it's critical to publicly recognize any time these improvements are achieved. Whereas promotion announcements can be divisive because they are pointing toward a zero-sum game, employee achievements are a completely different ballgame. Colleagues can rally around one another for personal achievements that they know their cohorts have worked for in a demonstrable manner. With this model everyone gets their own cheerleading squad. Beyond this, they can motivate others in the company to emulate. Not everyone can get a promotion, but everyone can get a certification or some sort of training that makes the entire team stronger. In one fell swoop, you have effectively built culture, a network of support, and are measurably bettering business and skills.

TYPES OF COACHING

Coaching can result in a lot of growth and resolve several problems. Throughout the Adaptive Experiment some high-level categories of coaching emerged.

UNLOCKING THE POTENTIAL OF RELATIONSHIPS

We have talked a lot about the human element of the workplace. In a typical company, the hierarchy encourages us to look at titles and roles, while humanity is overlooked and discounted in many ways. One of the primary ways in which companies dehumanize business is by either forcing or neglecting relationships. Coaching offers a method for alleviating these issues.

Friction and disengagement among employees occur. In a hierarchy, you do not *have* to care about relationships if you do not want to. There is nothing that requires social engagement. Many companies have team events, mixers, and holiday parties, and these are great for morale and interpersonal relationships. But they are a blunt instrument. In hierarchies, social engagement is optional; in the Adaptive model, it is required.

Organizational network analyses give you data to target engagement improvements. Engagement improvement makes the workplace happier, and I have also noticed a strong correlation between greater social cohesion and higher individual scores.

In a hierarchical company, broken relationships are ignored, making people miserable and decreasing productivity. Many times, no one even realizes these counterproductive relationships exist. Such problems can be resolved through coaching.

I worked with a guy we'll call Adam who had a master's degree from Stanford and wrote the code used to launch rockets. He's brilliant and invaluable to the company but lacks interpersonal skills.

People like Adam are easy to find in an organizational network analysis. They are often isolated, with only a few incoming links and few or no outgoing links. They do not have much empathy for their colleagues. On 360 feedback, they typically have a high IQ and atrocious EQ scores. Hierarchies protect people like this. Networks highlight them.

Coaches trained Adam how to better interact with his colleagues *and* coached his colleagues on how to better interact with Adam. In their book *Triggers: Creating*

Behavior That Lasts—Becoming the Person You Want to Be, Marshall Goldsmith and Mark Reiter write about understanding your own personal triggers for bad behavior and being open with colleagues about those triggers. In other words, it takes a village to crush counterproductive behavior. This kind of coaching creates greater empathy, a lack of which is often at the heart of workplace dysfunction. It is easy to dehumanize someone in the hierarchy, so in a transition to Adaptive you need to work to create empathy.

This was the problem with Adam *and* his colleagues. Adam was producing results that were hard to operate, and his colleagues were too intimidated by him to try to set him straight. By helping Adam better understand operational realities, we convinced him to make solutions that made his colleagues' lives easier. Likewise, Adam's colleagues learned to show him how to improve. In the absence of 360 feedback and an organizational network analysis, we might have never known the full extent of the animosity between these two parties.

UNLOCKING INDIVIDUAL POTENTIAL

Disengaged employees are a frequent problem in dysfunctional networks. These people punch their timecard and that's it. Engaging these employees requires making boring problems intensely interesting.

For instance, a colleague recommended I transfer Todd, a member of another department in the company, to my own. Todd wasn't happy where he was and had disengaged, but my colleague said Todd was amazing. After some arm twisting, Todd joined the Adaptive Experiment.

For the next six months, Todd refused to engage and his scores were low.

"You need to create a competition for Todd," my colleague told me. "Todd thrives when he feels like he's in a competitive race with someone."

You must be *incredibly careful* when introducing competition to a team. It must be clear the competition is for discovery and not judgment.

To stoke a competitive fire within Todd, I set up a hackathon. Almost immediately, Todd stepped up to the plate. He worked nights. He worked weekends. He was eventually responsible for authoring three different patent applications with my team. He consistently gets some of the best scores on the team and he is now a coach himself—all because we found a dynamic that engaged him.

You can find disengaged employees by looking for individuals who look great on paper but have low IQ and

EQ scores. They are qualified and should be crushing it but for some reason aren't. You need to have a heart-to-heart with them about what can get them engaged. Todd needed healthy competition, but there are many ways to motivate someone—sometimes you just have to ask. If they don't know, ask the team to brainstorm creative ways to engage the person.

NETWORK ADJUSTMENTS

No matter how creative you get, sometimes people are just in the wrong part of the network.

For instance, Marianne came to the Adaptive Experiment with exceptional credentials but performed abysmally. A fog of misery emanated from her. When I sat down with Marianne, I learned that she was imminently qualified in something other than what she had been asked to do!

We created a place in the network where Marianne could provide value. We paired her up with an extraordinarily nice guy. She thrived immediately. She thanked us, and her engagement increased significantly.

IDENTIFY AND REMOVE KEY PEOPLE RISKS

Many corporations employ individuals who are considered critical to the firm's success. The company believes it would sustain terrible losses if any of these key people were to leave. Some companies take out key-person insurance to blunt their losses if that key person dies or is severely injured. Many executives are considered key employees.

Key people stand out in an organizational network analysis. They have many incoming relationships that are frequent and high priority, even if they are not managers. In many ways, these key people hold a form of positional power. They are in place and cannot move, and many key people I meet are miserable and feel trapped.

What's more, they can behave in whatever way they want, which puts the entire team at risk. The difference between a key person and someone with anointed power is that key people have usually grown into their role by dint of their skill and long-term value to the company instead of having their status bestowed upon them.

The Adaptive model can reduce reliance on key people by creating redundancy in ways that hierarchies can't. A hierarchy would not have two heads of software engineering, for example, because that would create animosity or turf wars. An Adaptive organization, however, gives individuals the freedom to work on different things in addition to their redundant responsibilities, allowing the organization to maintain some redundancies without the conflict that often results.

One way for a company to reduce its reliance on a key employee is to send that person on vacation for two or three weeks and ask that they disconnect from work. The company can't contact them either, unless some existential risk arises.

This quickly unearths all the key-person problems so that the company can create more fluidity through shared responsibilities. The company can document the skills the key person provides and identify the skills it needs to add to the company even after the key employee returns. Key people often shepherd some arcane, manual process that could be automated by a bot and maybe a few machine-learning algorithms.

The idea of creating redundancy like this might sound expensive, but in the grand scheme of things, it is not. The alternative is unmanaged risk, which can be far more expensive.

If your margins are razor thin, automating a key employee's Rube Goldberg process might be a bridge too far. If you're in that situation, convince the key employee to delegate or redesign that process in a way that disincentivizes key-person behaviors.

As with anything else, you can climb any mountain by looking down and putting one foot in front of the other. All it takes to get started is one step.

BRINGING IN ISOLATED EMPLOYEES

Coaching helps individuals with few connections in the organizational network analysis. Having few connections is not always indicative of a problematic or unskilled employee. Sometimes, people have few connections because they are new to a team, introverted, or simply socially inept. We want to make room for this sort of diversity on the team because if someone has a superpower, it is up to the individual and the team to unlock it. Relative isolation can be alleviated through coaching. If someone is new to a team, they can be assigned a mentor to help them integrate. A coach can teach an employee how to engage with the team in ways that, while not entirely natural to the person, may still be feasible.

Many of us innately understand that building soft power includes things like talking about our kids and vacations or posting pictures of our dog. But not everyone gets this. Some people find personal discussions difficult, unnerving, or even distasteful. They might see these interactions as something that is reserved for their friends or family. In these scenarios, coaching might be as simple as encouraging someone to ask their coworkers about their family, dog, or hobby. The goal is to begin building up empathy for someone's personal life as well as professional life. While this might sound simplistic, some people need this type of guidance, and it has a positive impact on their engagement and connection within the team.

A very capable woman joined my team. She drove hard to achieve results, tended to dominate discussions, and had a small network as a result. For one quarter, her only team goal was to strengthen her influence in the network. She did what she does best and produced an amazing process to do so. She created a radar of all of the people she felt were critical to her success and the success of her team. She categorized and prioritized each relationship. She then produced a plan for how to strengthen each relationship and executed against that plan. She was fierce and wildly successful, becoming a far more influential person in the network.

Finding people like this in the network is easy. They typically have solid IQ and EQ scores but a small number of connections (sometimes just one or two). When you see team members like this, either their colleagues aren't providing them with feedback for some reason or they aren't well positioned to have greater influence in the network.

Team coaching may also be required. If you know two people work together, yet there wasn't any feedback from one of them, ask why. Work with the team to give that isolated coworker feedback so that it's easier for them to integrate. Encourage team members who could benefit from a relationship with that person to reach out.

EXPANSIVE COACHING

This variety of coaching is used on people who receive amazing IQ and EQ scores, with a low variance from quarter to quarter. In situations like this you need to look to expand the influence of those people who are performing very well. They clearly have superpowers that perhaps can be taught. Or they are stuck in a rut.

You might want to change their position in the network so they can try out new things. Often, this means their scores will dip for a while. That is not only okay, but good! You are looking to lower their scores by putting them in increasingly uncomfortable situations that they are excited about and that allow room to grow.

A few employees will put themselves in this type of position voluntarily, but as we discussed in the previous chapter, most will not due to the comfort of stasis. It is up to the coach to help the employee identify growth areas and to encourage them to push beyond comfort zones.

STRATEGIC COHESION COACHING

While all coaching should loop back to the strategic goals of a company, cohesion coaching is most aligned with universal company goals. While every company can hire new people to introduce new skills to an organization, it is always best to teach the most solid performers in the company new tricks and to level them up.

One of the things I built into the Adaptive Engagement Platform is the ability to align individuals with strategic change initiatives. This explicit alignment enables companies to see how cohesive the network is in supporting each change initiative. If you have a strong, tight-knit team that supports and trusts one another, then your chances of successfully executing on a strategic change initiative are better than with a weak, sparsely connected team.

Strategic cohesion coaching is all about improving the overall cohesion of the network aligned with a change initiative. There is a body of established graph analysis algorithms available to you in tools like Cytoscape that will enable you to measure the structural cohesion of the teams aligned with a particular change initiative. By understanding what this structural cohesion looks like, you can coach the team holistically to improve group dynamics and successfully execute a strategy.

Look at the strategic skills the organization feels are necessary and determine how prevalent those skills are in the aligned team. I refer to this as team strength. When those skills don't exist within the company, coaches should examine the tribe to determine who would be a good target for acquiring those strategic skills. The employee also must be interested in developing those skills. Once the agreement is made, the coach and employee will produce a plan, which might involve training or certification. The company pays for the employee to obtain these skills and supports the employee through the process.

You can improve cohesion by creating a shared personal improvement objective for the team, often based on books that strike at the heart of some of the themes that arise from the feedback. For example, if trust issues are damaging structural cohesion, consider a weekly book club on *The Speed of Trust: The One Thing That Changes Everything* by Stephen M. R. Covey. Another favorite is *The Five Dysfunctions of a Team: A Leadership Fable* by Patrick Lencioni. Listening and communication skills would be helpful? Consider *Just Listen: Discover the Secret to Getting Through to Absolutely Anyone* by Mark Goulston or *Crucial Conversations: Tools for Talking When Stakes Are High* by Kerry Patterson, et al. Struggling with operational hair balls? Look to *The Phoenix Project: A Novel about IT, DevOps, and Helping Your Business Win* by Gene Kim.

A weekly book club gives everyone a shared goal that is *not* directly related to work. This means it will have a lower chance of exacerbating existing tensions while getting everyone to work together sharing lessons from the book. It also sets up an accountability expectation that is critical for strengthening tribes. If a team member shows up without having read the prerequisite number of chapters, it offers a safe way to explore tribal accountability.

If speed is of the essence, consider hiring an outside consultancy that already has a team with the right dynamics. This will enable you to move forward on the tactical needs while building up the muscles necessary to address the strategic needs.

INTERPERSONAL COACHING

As I mentioned before, Ed Catmull, the author of *Creative, Inc.*, says that the most critical element of a collaborative team is the spirit in the room. Interpersonal coaching seeks to cultivate the best spirit possible and turns that quest into a collective endeavor.

This is far and away the most traditional form of coaching, focusing on the individual and their ability to operate in and strengthen an Adaptive organization. My favorite coaching books on helping people level up their interpersonal skills are *Triggers* and *What Got You Here Won't Get You There,* both by Marshall Goldsmith.

COACHING NEW HIRES

The same skill-based mindset in service to the company strategy that underlies coaching is also at the heart of the hiring process in a network organization. Rather than hiring for position titles, the company will hire based on skills necessary at that point in time.

Hiring for skill rather than position is more important now than ever before. In this age when technology is on hyperdrive, it's often more efficient to hire someone who already understands a new coding language and have them disseminate that information to the team than it is to teach someone on the team that skillset.

It would be almost impossible to rejigger a hierarchy fast enough to deal with today's competitive marketplace. While the management team is busy reorganizing their structure to accommodate someone new, they run the risk of getting sideswiped by a couple of kids from MIT who can destroy the company's market position in just a few weeks. Even more dangerous is that kids from IIT—the MIT of India—can also swipe your market position right from under you. Remember, there are billions of chances that someone is thinking about creatively destroying your company.

In a network organization, we can easily hire in such a way that we are able to focus on the market, rather than the business. It is about getting the right people into the right spots in order to capitalize on the market and technology as it stands *right now*—not three months from now.

Once you have named the skills you need, there are still some issues to overcome to successfully integrate new hires into your network. If you've seen the movie *Shawshank Redemption*, you remember the scene in which a prisoner who is released from jail at an elderly age ultimately takes his own life. He has been so conditioned to living in a restrictive environment that the freedom is too much for him. He is so overwhelmed at the notion of taking control of his own life that death feels like the more preferable option.

This is a dramatic analogy for the way many new employees experience the transition from a hierarchical organization to an Adaptive organization, but it is nevertheless apt. It never ceases to amaze me how long the adjustment period is for new employees who join a network organization after working at a hierarchical organization. Every person I have seen transition from a hierarchical to a network organization goes through a significant transition period.

It's best to assign new employees to a mentor for the first ninety days. Having a lightweight manager easing new hires into the Adaptive dynamic increases the chances of a successful integration. Bad scores for the new employee are okay—consider that part of the adjustment.

It took a while into the Adaptive Experiment to realize that we needed someone to help mentor new hires so that we could get past the deer-in-the-headlights phase faster. We eventually learned to get a volunteer who is *not* a coach to mentor new hires. This disperses critical servant-leadership and coaching skills and further mutes positional power within the org by democratizing the mentoring experience.

That initial mentor is responsible for much more than just career development; they are there to help the new employee get over the institutional shock of being part of a new model.

Many people have worked for hierarchical organizations for so long that they have developed institutionalized thinking and bring that with them into their new role. They are so used to being told what to do that they have effectively lost their sense of self-determination in a professional setting. Frequently, they feel lost because they don't have someone telling them what to do every day. In this case, the new hire's mentor will walk them through the adjustment period.

I once worked with a new hire who I thought wouldn't adjust to the Adaptive mentality. He could not break the habit of waiting to be told what to do before acting. We worked patiently with him for six months. I was concerned his scores would never improve, but then it clicked. He rediscovered his self-determination and helped our team produce two patent applications.

The new-hire mentor should try to identify opportunities for the new employee to build up soft power within the network by identifying the new hire's skills and passions and triangulating that with what needs to be done. The goal is to pick places where a new hire can demonstrate to their peer group that they are a valuable addition to the network.

When selecting these opportunities to build soft power and influence, choose a task or project that is not mission critical. A mission-critical objective can backfire by generating stress that can cause the employee to fail. Instead, look for projects that are self-contained, so that if the new hire messes up, no one else within the network is directly impacted. Tee up the ball so the employee gets a good hit. While the task may not generate a material result, the employee is racking up soft power, respect, and integration—and that's a good business result. The entire network is strengthened.

My favorite ninety-day starter project for new hires is cleaning up something that is a known mess but still works. If they completely miss, you can always fall back to the old way. If they succeed, they have contributed to the long-term health of the tribe and re-energized something burdensome. Furthermore, re-engineering some existing thing to be better is a fantastic learning experience.

It is also important to understand that not everyone will make it through this transitional process, even with a dedicated mentor. I once hired a young man who was also a new father, and who had recently moved his family to a new town to be near his elderly parents. Within a few weeks he came to me and said, "Chris, I can't hack it here."

"Why?" I asked.

This guy was fantastic and losing him was going to hurt. That said, he was the nervous sort and had assumed a lot of risk very quickly.

He said the pressure of having to make his own decisions

was just too great for him at that point in his life. He took a job with a property and casualty insurance company.

Remember, hierarchies call for social compliance and require employees to give up their practice of self-determination in the workplace. They exchange this for what many perceive as stability. Once the human brain begins to conflate these two things, it is an exceedingly difficult behavior to break.

IDENTIFYING YOUR COACHING STAFF

Now that we understand what coaching entails, who does it? When putting a coaching team together, the inclination of most companies is to shift those who were managers under the hierarchy into coaching positions. Some managers will make great coaches, but others will not. All of this is gauged on a person-by-person basis that requires analysis. Managers who operate with a servant-leader mentality often naturally and successfully shift into a coaching role. I have seen many companies surprised by how many natural servant leaders they have in place; the issue is that the organizational model didn't give those people the latitude and flexibility they needed to put those skills into action.

Other managers will not have a servant-leader mindset. If the hierarchy is going to remain largely in place but with a coaching program, it is sometimes possible to bring in an outside source who can train managers in coaching and servant-leadership skills that will allow them to cultivate soft power and learn to coach rather than manage their team. For some managers, this is a big—and even unbroachable—shift. Rather than directing the work of their team, under a coaching program they are charged with helping the team members manage themselves. This can be a difficult transition.

Coaches must understand the difference between coaching and managing. This difference is especially important to highlight if a former manager is put in a coaching position. It can be all too easy to perform the same function under a new title. Whereas a manager will assign tasks and control a team of direct reports, a coach serves as a mentor. Coaching does not involve telling people what to do; it is doing everything possible to guide team members toward maximizing their potential and being the best version of themselves.

COACHING VERSUS MANAGING

One of the most difficult things for people to understand is that coaching is not managing. Managers often feel the need to personally make quick decisions, and that urgency costs them the opportunity to teach individuals to work together to make fast, viable decisions. Coaching involves teaching. In this process, team members learn but so do the coaches. In every way, the team and company are stronger with this type of program in place.

I began managing in 1999. I was trained in traditional management techniques, including annual reviews, HR processes, gang charts, and more. My mother gave me a copy of *The One Minute Manager* by Ken Blanchard, which I dutifully read. This book is still one of the best management books around. Then I settled into giving directions, coordinating work, completing annual reviews, and tackling HR issues.

I was a terrible manager. I chafed at the repetitive administrative work. I hated being a manager but I was, and always have been, a fierce servant leader. I get an amazing rush when I can cheer a team to success. I have a deep well of experience, dating back to when I first started programming in 1979, that I can leverage to help people succeed.

When I started the Adaptive Experiment in 2013, I made a conscious decision *not* to be a manager. I have always tried to automate away boring tasks or to otherwise alter them to make them fun. I suppose creating an army of bots to free me from the burden of being a manager so that I could focus on servant leadership is what led to the Adaptive Engagement Platform.

Even after making this commitment and acknowledging that I was a terrible manager, I continually found myself making managerial decisions. To accomplish a task, a manager will break that task down, assign the work, then ride herd over the team until the task is done. This can be fast and efficient, but it also denies the team an opportunity to figure out how to do things. Contemporary management denies employees the opportunity to grow and mature, keeping them in a state of career adolescence. There is no trust or empathy required.

As a servant leader, the objective is to coach a team so that they can break down the work themselves, figure out who is in the best position to complete the work, and then hold each other accountable to complete the task. This is tactically slower but yields strategic speed over time. Managers do not need patience. Servant leaders do.

Blanchard also authored a fantastic book on servant leadership titled *Servant Leadership in Action: How You Can Achieve Great Relationships and Results* that I encourage every coaching program to require as mandatory reading.

Even if your company doesn't have a coaching program, chances are you already have coaches on your team. You just might not be aware of it. Organizational network analysis may demonstrate that you already have soft-power brokers with a lot of connections who serve as a positive, connecting force and a natural source of motivation and feedback. Regardless of their stature within the hierarchy, beloved and respected employees are the ones you want on your coaching team.

COACHES—THEY WALK AMONG US

Your organizational network analysis from the 360 analyses is the map you need to find your coaches. The best coaches have between six and eight inbound connections and about the same number of outgoing connections. This indicates they are both receiving and writing a lot of feedback. In effect, they are already acting as coaches. They also have great IQ and EQ scores with a low variance for at least three quarters. The definition of "great" is up to you, as is the definition of "low variance." The feedback they get should be authentic and critical. This demonstrates that their colleagues do not feel the need to exercise any fear-based glad-handing.

The best coaches also have a solid portfolio of acquired skills. They have deep experience in some part of the industry and can speak authoritatively about a subject. They often have experience talking about the subject, either because they speak at conferences, have authored papers about it, or frequently speak on the topic within the company. They also have a solid understanding of the team and business. They understand how to combine team members in specific ways to cover one another's weaknesses and accentuate strengths.

Once you have found a well-connected and skilled coaching staff, make sure they are up to the task. Volunteerism is a big part of a successful Adaptive organization. You want team members to volunteer for projects and tasks because it allows them to exercise self-determination and work on things that fulfill and excite them. Coaching should be the same way; a person should be qualified for coaching, but just as important is their interest in coaching. You must clarify with each potential coach that they are willing to invest in coaching and guiding every person on their team.

Your company can also establish a coaching certification program for anyone who volunteers to coach. Becoming a certified coach should be treated as a personal improvement objective just like any other. Log it in your work-management system and then find a program you can use to get people trained. Sites like Udemy provide a lot of options. I recommend everyone get a copy of *Servant Leadership in Action*.

Your coaches should continue to perform their day-to-day functions in addition to coaching. Many managers lose the muscles needed to deliver the concrete results they ask of their team. I contend that if coaches can't do the same work as those they coach, they won't have the street cred to help the person they are coaching level up. In the Adaptive Experiment, everyone contributed concrete results to the team, even me. I was responsible for writing the code for the Adaptive Engagement Platform, prototyping new architectural designs, and interfacing with the executive team. Only the first two earned me street cred with the people I was coaching.

Coaching is more science than art. If your company is shifting from a hierarchical model to an Adaptive network, it is possible your new coaches have never seen coaching in practice before. For this reason, allow new coaches to ride shotgun with more seasoned coaches if you have them. If you don't have any seasoned coaches and aren't willing to wing it, there are scads of great coaches you can hire for a quarter or two to show you the ropes. Such an apprenticeship program will give new coaches a feel for what coaching entails. You will provide your coaches with guidelines before they get started, but nothing is as illustrative as watching a skilled coach in practice.

COACHING FEEDBACK

A coaching program is only as effective as its coaches. Team-member feedback on each coach will help ensure your coaching program remains strong. In the survey, ask team members how effective their coaches were over the course of the previous quarter. Did they help you level up? Did they teach you something?

It is up to the coaching staff to act on survey results. If a coach falls below an established score over a series of consecutive quarters, they should be removed from the coaching team. This is another difference between managing and coaching—there is no established positional power. You become and remain a coach only if you are effective.

In Adaptive, being removed from the coaching program is not a failure. A person is removed from coaching merely because the numbers dictate it, and there should be no stigma attached to the change. In fact, someone removed from the coaching team would receive resources to continue building the skills they already have—skills that make the entire group stronger.

A hierarchical company often puts people on ladder rungs they are not suited for. You may have seen this: Terry is amazing at his job and he's been at the company for a long time. The company rewards him by making him a manager. The problem is that Terry is horrible at it. In many companies, Terry would either linger as a bad manager or be fired. In those scenarios, everyone loses; the once-amazing Terry is now unemployed and the company no longer has Terry's original skillset.

SAMPLE COACHING SURVEY QUESTIONS

Here are some of the questions we asked our coaches during the Adaptive Experiment that you may find helpful in your own coaching program.

How satisfied were you with this person's coaching skills over the last quarter?

- Did they help you see strengths or weaknesses that you had not previously seen?

- Were they able to give you advice that helped you improve?

- Do you feel like their skill and experience were assets to you?

How satisfied were you with your coach's reliability over the last quarter?

- Did they meet with you regularly?

- Do you feel they dedicated enough time for your conversations?

- Do you feel they were truly committed to helping you throughout the quarter?

Did they help you create actionable personal improvement goals for the quarter and hold you accountable for completing them?

WHEN COACHING DOES AND DOESN'T WORK

Many people respond well to coaching—even employees who are failing and dragging the team down. Others try to improve but cannot. Some just freeze. You will experience many versions of all these scenarios over time.

Let us return to the mysterious case of Marianne who was widely disliked. After several rounds of feedback, I spoke to her team leader about the situation. "I've known Marianne for more than twenty years and she's *always* been miserable," he said.

I thought, but did not say, "There's another common denominator in this, and it's you."

When I repositioned Marianne in the network, I hypothesized that she would blossom. Most people want to do great work, and when forced to do crappy work, they become disengaged.

When you make a move like this, emphasize to the employee that it's not punishment. Although parallel moves in a hierarchy are usually negative, shifts in an Adaptive network are about recognition and optimization. A person is not being kicked off a team, but put into a new position where they can offer more, be reinvigorated, and get a new opportunity to shine. It's important that the person agrees to move; without that consent, all you have done is gone another round in the destructive cycle of brainwashing people into abdicating self-determination.

I explained this to Marianne and she agreed a change was worth a try. I found a spot for her where she could work on something she told me she was interested in alongside an individual I knew to be a powerful coach. After twenty years of being miserable in the same department with the same company, Marianne is now happier than she has ever been.

Previously, no one talked to Marianne about her discontent or put her in a different position. Coaching revealed she was in the wrong place and led to a transformation.

This is not always the case. A team member, Ned, is a good example.

I loved Ned; he was hilarious and a good friend of mine. Unfortunately, he could not get over the threshold we needed him to. Despite three rounds of coaching, he continued to perform poorly and his colleagues rated him low. Ned was headstrong and convinced that he was awesome while everyone else just could not appreciate his genius. Had he just been willing to listen or tried different ways of achieving his goals, he would have been awesome.

Ned's numbers never improved. His team was not confident in his performance. In situations like this, you must honor the numbers and move or remove people who are not performing up to the standards set by the company.

The minute you violate this trust, the team will decide that the organization is not truly flat or fluid.

If you violate that trust even once, it will take you an exceptionally long time to earn it back. In the end, I had to honor the numbers and terminate Ned's employment. I still go to dinner with him whenever I am in his neck of the woods.

CHAPTER EIGHT

COMMON HURDLES

———

I have seen how much is gained from setting up even some of the Adaptive model in companies. Moving from hierarchy to a flat and fluid model like Adaptive is not always smooth, but most companies can overcome the obstacles to become a more Adaptive organization.

I have seen network organizations work in the most unlikely environment of them all: India. For many, the only viable career move in much of India is one that leads to a management position. The status that comes from a management position means that droves of people who have no business managing anyone are driving hard to become a manager. When I talk with my Indian colleagues about the horror stories I have heard about in the United States, they laugh. "You are an amateur until you work for an Indian manager," a friend of mine once said to me.

When I set up Adaptive organizations in India, I had to be cognizant of the social restrictions the model challenges. While a few Indian participants in the Adaptive Experiment struggled with their newly found autonomy, these problems were minor and fleeting. The greatest challenge was breaking through to human resources executives. Indian HR teams harbor a parent-child-like view of their employees; HR treats employees like immature wards rather than professionals.

Despite this challenging mindset, the Adaptive model works better in India than in America because the culture is inherently more collaborative than competitive. The challenge in India is getting buy-in for the network idea. Once that is accomplished, some of my biggest success stories are out of India.

This is all to say: if a two-thousand-year-old culture can break out of an ingrained mindset, chances are your company can too.

WHEN THINGS GO WRONG

If you are moving your organization to an Adaptive model and encountering problems, it could be because many people see this model as their enemy rather than their friend.

People are usually in favor of a flat and fluid organization when they read about it or stumble across a culture doc created by a tribal company. But the support can change once people start the process. After several rounds of feedback and scoring, some companies see engagement going down and negative energy within the team on the rise. This indicates something has gone off-course.

If you see this trend, step in and troubleshoot. In this chapter, we will look at some of the most common barriers to overcome when rolling out a network organization.

THE SILO MINDSET

This is the single most common and trickiest hurdle companies must contend with when breaking out of a hierarchy to become more Adaptive. Without even realizing it, people become stuck in the hierarchy mindset. One of the most effective ways to begin combating institutionalization is through communication platform technologies like Slack or MS Teams.

Traditional email systems create silos through functionalities such as CC and BCC. Furthermore, email threads tend to create habit trails for people who use "reply all" to hijack the thread for a different topic, same group. The pain of administering email groups forces this kind of behavior. Slack cuts through the organization and begins to create a naturally transformative effect in which people collaborate on things in ways that they normally wouldn't.

Like all technologies, Slack will someday be outmoded. What will not change is the utilization of a fluid collaboration model. If anything, Slack will be replaced by something even more fluid and collaborative. The point here is that to move forward, companies need a technology that enables them to rapidly bring together groups of people and align them toward a purpose. Installing group chat technologies into business serves as the foundation for a cooperative and collaborative environment because it creates rapid alignment, independent of the hierarchy.

My recommendation for overcoming this issue is to create a strong rollout strategy for the collaboration platform of your choice. Get everyone on board. The executives, primarily, should be raving fans of the platform and abandon email for all internal communication. For example, a friend of mine became the president of a large company after a massive merger. He told the entire company that if anyone wanted to contact him, they could do it through Slack because he would not respond to email. His implicit message was that to successfully merge monster companies requires the transparency and silo-busting that only a robust collaboration platform can deliver.

DISENGAGED MANAGERS

Moving toward a network organization requires that everyone buys into and collaborates in the process. In the case of a disengaged manager or a manager who enjoys their positional power and the benefits that come with it, you will not have the ingredients necessary to institute the essential element of servant leadership.

Moving forward in the face of a lack of buy-in from managers will only do damage overall. I have seen it happen before: a company introduces the idea of feedback and coaching. Employees get excited about the prospect of change and providing good, actionable feedback for their colleagues. They open their hearts, pour their souls out, and then—crickets. No action is taken. Nothing really changes, because managers have not bought in and are dismissive of the process. Employees end up feeling worse than they did to begin with because they allowed themselves to be vulnerable. It creates an even *worse* situation because now employees *know* that management is aware of their problems and frustrations but *still* does not want to lift a finger to fix them. The truth has been exposed to employees, and it is not a pretty truth.

It is okay to decide that a company does not have the infrastructure or people in place necessary to make the jump to a flatter, more fluid model. However, it is critical that your company comes to this understanding *before* attempting to embark upon instituting one. If the people who need to be on board to make Adaptive work haven't bought in, train them to be servant leaders through executive coaching (which doesn't work for everyone), replace them with a servant leader, or don't even try to walk this road in the first place.

Begin by having a heart-to-heart with all the company's managers at your next leadership event. Talk with them about the importance of servant leadership, growing employees, and scaling trust and empathy. Those who are willing to take the leap should be rewarded with an opportunity to become a coach. Invest in those initial volunteers because they really care. If you are committed to becoming an Adaptive servant-leadership organization, you may find that some of your managers cannot make the leap.

I once rolled out Adaptive for a new, large, and sprawling team. I met with the manager, who was surprisingly gung-ho to transition. We taught people how to give great feedback and interact with the Adaptive Engagement Platform bots. Then, the platform launched the first round of 360s.

The results were jaw-dropping. This team was a mess. The network of feedback we collected was sparsely connected. There was a lot of animosity within the team. Most strikingly, the manager received only two pieces of feedback, and they were not positive. The HR professionals rolling out the model decided people didn't understand how to use the bot, even though we had successfully rolled out Adaptive to other teams without any training.

We held another round of training to emphasize the importance of helping colleagues level up. Then the platform ran another round of 360s and received a similar response. The group was fragmented with several low-performing team members.

There was one exception.

One team was led by an immigrant from Vietnam whose language skills were challenged, and I am being polite. This manager grilled me about the nuances of the bot, servant leadership, and how to give valuable feedback. After the first round of feedback, his team was just as fragmented and weak as the rest of the group. The second round showed dramatic improvement, and conversations with his team indicated their leader had made a lot of improvements. It turns out the one person I did not think would be a good servant leader was a great one.

Meanwhile, his manager, the one who had been so gung-ho for his department to make this transition, received just a smattering of feedback and terrible scores once again in the second round. He accused the people running the Adaptive Experiment of rigging the system against him. In fact, he went as far as to approach everyone on his team to ask them if they had provided him with feedback. He demonstrated beyond any doubt that he was not a servant leader. Most of his team was disbanded and reassigned, which yielded a far more healthy, productive, and collaborative group.

DISSATISFIED EMPLOYEES

Employees who do not like their jobs can pose a major sticking point in Adaptive organizations. Unfortunately, this is something you cannot fix—you cannot force a team member to like their job if they are in the wrong job to begin with or in it just for the paycheck. You cannot force this type of employee to suddenly give a damn.

What this model *will* do is unmask those employees. It will reveal deep, structural problems such as this one, which companies must get past before an Adaptive model can be successfully applied.

The organizational network analysis will act as an X-ray into your business, allowing you to see the lay of the land and figure out where the hard and soft spots are. You may discover you have a bunch of people who do not like each other, aren't engaged, or don't like what they're doing.

The Adaptive model will not fix this. All of this must be resolved *before* you delve any deeper.

In her book *Primed to Perform*, Lindsay McGregor talks about the social engineering necessary to motivate a team. It turns out that this is not what most people think. She identifies six motivating factors, three of which are productive and three that are not. The three productive motivating factors are play (doing something because you love it), purpose, and potential. The three counterproductive motivating factors are emotional pressure (from negative emotions such as disappointment, guilt, or shame), economic pressure, and inertia, or fear of change.

Independent of creating an Adaptive organization, create a strategy that allows you to transition away from the counterproductive motivating factors and toward productive motivating factors. This should get your company to a place where most people who are internally driven to do an excellent job and deliver greatness are enthusiastic.

For most companies, this will be enough to begin a transition to a more Adaptive organization. Most companies have a bunch of employees who are feeling downtrodden because they have been fighting "the man" for years. Functioning under this mindset requires a lot of energy, which eats up the attention they could otherwise be putting into creating their best work. Deep down, employees like this are intrinsically motivated to do an excellent job. Since most people fit into this category, providing them with the token motivation necessary to enhance their work experience unlocks a ton of pent-up potential. From here, you are better able to identify the truly and intrinsically disengaged employees, who simply need to go for this model to work.

COMPETITION

Internal competition erodes the Adaptive model because it runs counter to trust and empathy. It is hard to trust someone who is in competition with you. In some companies, team members are competing with one another for work. This often happens in sales and sometimes in research teams. It is difficult to collaborate in this type of environment because the system has been designed in such a way that individual contribution is king, and collaboration can hurt your competitive edge. Clearly, collaboration runs contrary to competition, and collaboration is at the heart of a successful network.

I once worked with a team in India that I had been warned hated one another. Then I began collecting their 360 feedback and realized that wasn't true at all. They were all either complimenting one another or providing solid, actionable feedback about ways in which their team members could improve. Confusingly, their scores did not match their feedback. One employee might compliment another team member in the written feedback, then proceed to hammer that person with a low score in the same category. At first, I could not figure out what was going on. Clearly, there was a big disconnect.

Finally, I sat the team down as a group and asked for some insight. Crickets. After several seconds of awkward silence, one of the team members looked at me and said, "Perhaps you will get better answers if you talk to us individually." He was right. On their own, each one of these team members told me that they competed with one another; it followed that getting rid of high-performing colleagues opened up more opportunity for each one of them as individuals.

It was a cut-throat strategy, but many industries work like that. Still, in general, most companies will achieve better results by figuring out how to take advantage of the fifty thousand years' worth of genetic programming that has made human beings collaborative creatures. Our survival as the apex species of the planet did not come because of our individual performance. In the grand scheme of things, as individuals we are all pretty soft and weak. If you do not believe me, go a few rounds with a jaguar or try to survive the extreme conditions in which Tardigrades find themselves. Human beings prosper from the competitive advantage that comes from working together.

Some companies disagree—they want to breed internal competition. Admittedly, this can sometimes be productive. For example, if members of the same team have very strong but differing opinions about how to solve a problem, I'll often work with them to devise an inexpensive competitive experiment to test the merits of different approaches. The result will be a proven approach and the losing team now joins the winning team.

Other times, competition can be insanely damaging, specifically when it damages psychological safety. I've seen this happen most often when I've been brought in to help a company develop a next-generation software platform to replace a legacy solution, often built using very old technologies. Here, the implication is that the losing team (legacy technology) will not be joining the winning team (modern technology). Instead they will be joining the ranks of unemployment because their skills have not kept pace with the market. This creates animosity and damages empathy and trust on an industrial scale.

Sears CEO Eddie Lampert thought blood-sport competition would make Sears a stronger company. I have spoken with several people who worked in influential positions within Sears and witnessed Lampert pitting division against division. Because there was no opportunity for the losers to join the winners, the entire exercise was insanely damaging.

It *is* possible to change from a competitive environment to a collaborative one. The competitive team I described earlier that had mysteriously low numbers? We decided to change the dynamic of how they worked from competitive to collaborative. Over time, every individual on the team turned into a mini servant leader who helped their colleagues level up. The entire team matured from competitive islands to a group of people with extensive practical experience in providing one another with feedback based on practical experience. The team became more adaptive and agile, which allowed the entire company to transition and shift with more ease and to enjoy new business opportunities.

GAMING THE SYSTEM

If you implement the Adaptive model without thinking it through, it might result in a bunch of people gaming the system through false positive reviews. Invariably, every business leader I work with to establish a network model asks, "Well, won't they just give each other good scores?" The answer is, yes, that could happen.

In my six years running the Adaptive Experiment, I never saw even a whiff of this behavior. I suspect that this was, in part, because of the culture we had implemented that put integrity front and center in the narrative we wrote. I was once talking with the chief transformation officer for a large financial services company. He told me that they had abandoned their feedback system.

At one point, an IT guy came into this CTO's office, closed the door, and said, "Here's the deal: you give me a good score and I'll give you one."

Taken aback, I asked, "Did you call him out on his low-integrity behavior?"

"No," the CTO replied.

So much for transforming the company.

If you have a weak culture that tolerates low-integrity behavior, you have organizational debt that is rotting your company from the inside out.

If you are truly concerned that your team members will game the system, well, your house is on fire. Put this book down, go put out the fire, then come pick it up again.

Seriously. Go now. I can wait.

HIERARCHICAL INDUSTRIES

There are a few industries in which the hierarchy is too entrenched to overcome. Whereas a network may or may not work on a company-by-company basis in many industries, there are a few industries in which a hierarchy is pervasive across the board. The medical industry is a notable example of this. In medicine, there is a long and storied history of showing fealty to the doctor. Meanwhile, nurses were treated like second-class citizens.

Industries like this are exceedingly difficult to crack with a network because the culture is simply too ingrained. I would go as far as to say that, chances are, a network just will not work.

I remember speaking with a doctor who oversaw a large provider network. He said that he remembered his predecessor holding a town hall and talking about annual reviews. One of the nurses asked, "When do we get to provide feedback to our boss about the ways we would like them to improve?"

"You don't," he responded. "This isn't a circular firing squad."

Remind me not to work there!

THE ADAPTIVE REDSHIFT EFFECT

Earlier I wrote about an effect I saw enough times that I finally put a name to it—the "Adaptive Redshift Effect."

Redshift is a phenomenon in astronomy where light is stretched out into longer waves, which humans perceive as red. This is often caused by celestial bodies racing away from each other, which is exactly what happens with Adaptive teams inside of hierarchical organizations.

The dynamic is simple to understand and detect, though difficult to ameliorate. Because everyone in an Adaptive team is:

- on a personal improvement plan
- given full autonomy to take part in complex collaboration patterns to solve big problems in whatever way they see fit
- receiving regular feedback on how to level up

Adaptive teams evolve so much more rapidly than their colleagues in the broader organization. Before long, the Adaptive team looks like robots from the future while everyone else is stuck in place.

This dynamic can cause all sorts of problems. Key among them is jealousy. While team members in an Adaptive team cheer each other's accomplishments as they churn through their individual development objectives quarter after quarter, their colleagues in the hierarchy feel jealousy because they have not been afforded a similar opportunity.

The Adaptive team can also be something quite terrifying to people who are perfectly happy to be disengaged. They are here for a paycheck and have no desire to improve themselves. I'm not here to judge these people. They often have something else going on in their lives that requires as much energy as they can muster and so need their working lives to be on autopilot.

Finally, because Adaptive teams are evolving at a much faster clip than the rest of the company, they can soon appear to be alien in their ways. This can open up a cultural chasm that is hard to close.

If rolling out Adaptive to the entire company is not in the cards, I recommend adopting Adaptive in a team that can accommodate some sort of rotation schedule. For example, R&D teams can serve as a form of *dōjō*. This is from Wikipedia:

> A dōjō is a hall or space for immersive learning or meditation. This is traditionally in the field of martial arts, but has been seen increasingly in other fields, such as meditation and software development. The term literally means 'place of the Way' in Japanese."

So, people from the hierarchy can join the R&D team running Adaptive to solve some big problem, and then rotate out. I call this the "Netarchy," or the place where the hierarchy and Adaptive network overlap. People in the Netarchy would receive the same feedback and bot support as people in Adaptive. They worked in a dual operating system for how work got done. This worked exceptionally well over the years but did have one noticeable downfall: *people didn't want to leave the Adaptive team to return to their hierarchical team.*

EXPERIMENTATION IS KEY

Even with the best of intentions, not every attempt to create a flatter, more fluid organization will work. That is okay—the Adaptive model challenges structure, mindset, and process. You may try certain things and find they do not work for your company. Or you may realize that some elements of a network work for you while others do not. More important than creating a perfectly aligned and collaborative network is paying attention, listening, and acting when things are not working or can be improved. When practiced consistently, this kind of striving will make your company a happier, more productive place to be.

One of the greatest lessons I learned while running the Adaptive Experiment was that it enabled me to do just that—experiment. Experimenting based on empirical evidence on a flat, fluid team is far easier than experimenting on a hierarchy. Remember, hierarchies are incredibly rigid, brittle, and political. People with positional power are quick to feel threatened whenever they believe their turf is threatened. That turf, of course, is people. We often attribute status to people with very large teams. How often have you seen a phrase such as "I oversaw a division of five hundred people" on a resume or LinkedIn? In an era of ever more powerful and sophisticated machine-learning algorithms and robotics, I wonder how much longer this attitude will persist?

With Adaptive organizations, the only turf an employee possesses is the skills they have, their contributions, and their influence within the network. This makes experimentation far easier.

The Adaptive Experiment included hundreds of hypotheses, experiments, and adjustments. When I think back on where I started and where I ended up, it is breathtaking. It is this kind of rapid experimentation that can help every company create a continuous stream of improvements and ensure that you always stay flat, fluid, and adaptive.

CONCLUSION

___

On some level, we *all* know that business as usual is no longer working. If it were, we wouldn't be incessantly joking about workplace culture and watching executives drive their companies into the ground. We wouldn't all be so miserable at work. Businesses wouldn't be in such a constant scramble to keep up with the world around them.

There is no escaping the fact that a new model of business is essential for most of us. Otherwise, we will exist in a constant state of fear about being taken out by a competitor as opposed to coming together to solve the next big problem.

The model I am suggesting resolves—or at least alleviates—many of our problems. It offloads the administrative work of running an Adaptive team to bots so that we can get back to being human with one another. It allows employees to feel that their contribution matters; it makes work a more fulfilling, human experience; and it provides companies with an edge. It allows them to adapt more quickly and nimbly in ways that drive genuine business results. It enables companies to use quickly sophisticated collaboration models to align and adjust every person in the company with the ever-changing landscapes around them, putting to best use the resources they already have at their disposal.

Now that you have read all of this, I hope you will take a moment to stop and look around. Ask yourself if any of the scenarios in this book resonate with you. Do you see any of the hierarchical elements we discussed at play in your own company in a way that damages or inhibits its true potential? Do people make fun of their managers or bosses? Do they hang up posters of the Steve Jobs quote, "We don't hire smart people to tell them what to do, we hire smart people so they can tell us what to do"? These might seem like trivial things, but they are usually indicators of big problems in an environment where team members feel like they do not have a voice.

They are all signs pointing you to the fact that something is not right.

Stop and ask yourself how your company arrived at this point of being a hierarchical organization in the first place.

What have you lost along the way with all this arbitrary structure? What problems do you see today that might be a direct result of your current structure and organization? Be honest here: in what ways are you seeing positional power harm your company and the experience of those people who work within it?

Underlying everything we have discussed throughout this book is the idea that people *can* be happy and productive at work. Perhaps not every day but, across the board, people can feel satisfied and generally good about the time and energy they dedicate to their jobs. There is something deeply satisfying to humans about solving big problems through collaboration. This shouldn't be a novel idea—but it is.

A few years ago, I read an eye-opening book about the meaning of work. The book argued that America had settled into a Protestant work ethic—that happiness doesn't matter because God respects the work. It is through work that we show our dedication to God. We don't explain work in these terms in the modern day, but this is the mindset around which our thoughts about work have been formulated. Happiness is not for today, but for the afterlife. For decades, this has left too many people with the *expectation* that they are not going to be happy at work.

In the past ten years, we have seen a revolutionary idea

take hold that happiness *should* come into play at work. A quick Google search will yield hundreds of peer-reviewed studies and books on this very subject. If employees feel they can be happier elsewhere, they will seek that out.

People are also now seeking self-determination in the workplace. Those of us who are older may chaff at this attitude, but a young, mobile workforce is driving this trend, and innovative technologies are enabling new ways of managing companies to accommodate them. Either way you cut it, this is yet another reason why most companies need to shift to a more humanistic organizational model and away from the mechanical business philosophy. If you want employees to stay, you have to offer them fulfillment in their work environment. Self-determination is part of that.

You need a system that will allow you to quickly integrate and shed employees in a way that reduces risk to your businesses. A network model allows for both things. The truth is that no matter how much happiness and fulfillment you offer, the days of employees staying with one company throughout their career are gone.

When I started the Adaptive Experiment, I had no idea what kind of impact it would have on my life. The idea of using technology to terraform Adaptive companies filled with high-performing teams sounded idealistic, but in 2013 I thought that all of the elements were readily available: AWS for scalable infrastructure, powerful work-management tools, and, of course, new collaboration platforms that enabled people to work with bots as though they were people.

What ended up happening was that the Adaptive Engagement Platform and its quirky collection of bots enabled me to be more human. The bots I built took over facilitating the feedback process, helped employees with work discipline, and provided me with an immense amount of data. Where I was blind before, now I could see. This enabled me to make surgical improvements as opposed to using blunt-force trauma to improve the organization. Said more crassly, the bots took over all of the nagging and I was able to focus on coaching employees to level up their game. I was suddenly the good cop! For the first time in my professional career I suddenly had a lot of time on my hands to coach others. Self-directed, flat, fluid, and adaptive teams can fend for themselves.

When I had made the decision to start my own company based on this experiment, I decided I had an amazing opportunity to perform one last experiment. *What would happen if you shut it all down?*

It turns out...you can't.

The Adaptive Experiment participants have moved on to new opportunities, and every last one of them has reached out to me to convey how much of an impact the experiment had on them, both personally and professionally. Many of them continue to coach each other. The general theme from them all was that the trust and empathy they felt when they were part of the experiment helped them grow more and faster than at any other point in their careers.

Who would have thought that a bunch of quirky bots could help us all feel human again?

ACKNOWLEDGMENTS

I will start with wife, Heather, and daughter, Hannah, who demonstrated a level of patience and understanding that is hard to put into words. Heather not only listened; she helped me hone my thinking to a degree that made this book possible. Heather also happens to be an award-winning speech therapist who helped me design the dialogue engine for my bots.

Next, I would like to thank my mother, Diane Creel, who helped me fund the development of this book with her mother and my grandmother, LaFran Wallick. I would also like to thank my father, Richard Creel, an author himself who helped me with editing and funding.

I also owe a debt of gratitude to the extensive list of executives who gave me a chance to use their organizations as a lab to further my research and mentored me along the way. Two executives stand out—Dave Beaulieu and Doug Williams. Doug and Dave created an environment for me that enabled me to complete the years-long applied R&D necessary to unlock the discoveries I write about in this book. Without them, this book would be an academic puff piece or not exist at all.

Valerie Usilton, who wrote the foreword to this book, played a huge role in the Adaptive Experiment. She coached me every step of the way to ensure that the model served the needs of my human resources partners. Despite the apparent insanity of what I was doing, she kept an open mind throughout and gave me regular feedback to help me on the journey. She also helped me as a professional, giving me world-class coaching that made me a better leader.

My partners in building the Adaptive Engagement Platform also deserve my thanks. Bharath Kumar lent his development genius to the effort, yielding a result beyond my expectations. He is one of the finest developers I've ever known, and I am so grateful he agreed to join me.

Rob Held, Ryan Colleary, and Zack Walmer all helped me understand these ideas even more deeply, yielding a better book and platform. Their strategic genius helped me see the holistic nature of the Adaptive model and its power. Jamie Wasserman helped me finally understand the psychological implications, yielding an even more beneficial result.

The coaching team who worked with me during the last five years of the Adaptive Experiment were instrumental in helping me create the first version of the Adaptive Engagement Platform. Quarter after quarter they helped level up everyone on the team and the model itself. So, thank you, Chris Watson, Mykel Alvis, and William Vestal.

My biggest thanks go to the many people who participated in the Adaptive Experiment. These participants gave me critical feedback along the way that helped me course correct when I got lost and see the path more clearly when they felt I was on to something. It was at their urging that I wrote this book. The list of participants is long indeed, so my thanks to everyone who participated. A special thanks to the following people, all of whom played an instrumental role in making the platform and book happen: Akanksha Singh, Arseniy Zhizhelev, Bill Carlson, Byron Lagrone, Clarence Alston, Colleen Sullivan, Colleen Truppo. Daniel Strebel, Lisa Craig, Mallikarjun Peasarla, Matthew Dougherty, Mark Pomager, Nancy Patin, Nord Samuelson, Rebecca Strojan Weaver, Stephanie Pazniokas, and Vedratna Velani.

I will conclude with my humble thanks to Nikki Van Noy. When I first started working on this book in 2017, I quickly realized that I was in way over my head. I thought of myself as a pretty compelling author of articles and blogs. I have learned that has little to do with authoring a great book. It is like the difference between quantum mechanics and Newtonian physics. Nikki was the pro who helped me pull together a great book. Thank you, Nikki!

BIBLIOGRAPHY

I am so deeply grateful to the many authors who came before me who authored books the likes of which I can only aspire to write. I have mentioned several of these books above, each of which helped me tremendously in my journey. I list them below for your convenience, and I encourage you to read every one of them.

1. *Valve Employee Handbook* (https://www.valvesoftware. com/en/publications)
2. Arena, M. J. (2018). *Adaptive Space: How GM and Other Companies Are Positively Disrupting Themselves and Transforming into Agile Organizations.* New York: McGraw-Hill Professional.
3. Blanchard, K. H., Broadwell, R., & Maxwell, J. C. (2018). *Servant Leadership in Action: How You Can Achieve Great Relationships and Results.* Oakland, CA: Berrett-Koehler.
4. Catmull, E., & Wallace, A. (2015). *Creativity, Inc.*

Overcoming the Unseen Forces That Stand in the Way of True Inspiration. New York: Random House.

5. Christensen, C. M. (2011). *The Innovator's Dilemma.* New York: Harper Business.

6. Covey, S. M. (2006). *The Speed of Trust.* New York: Free Press.

7. Cross, R. L., & Parker, A. (2010). *The Hidden Power of Social Networks: Understanding How Work Really Gets Done in Organizations.* Boston: Harvard Business School Press.

8. Doshi, N., & McGreggor, L. (2015). *Primed to Perform: How to Build the Highest Performing Cultures through the Science of Total Motivation.* New York: Harper Business.

9. Friedman, T. L. (2007). *The World Is Flat.* London: Picador.

10. Goldsmith, M. (2007). *What Got You Here Won't Get You There: How Successful People Become Even More Successful.* New York: Hachette Books.

11. Goldsmith, M. (2016). *Triggers.* New York: Crown Business.

12. Goulston, M. (2015). *Just Listen: Discover the Secret to Getting Through to Absolutely Anyone.* New York: AMACOM.

13. Kim, G., Behr, K., & Spafford, G. (2018). *The Phoenix Project: A Novel about IT, DevOps, and Helping Your Business Win.* Portland, OR: IT Revolution Press.

14. Kotter, J. P. (2014). *Accelerate: Building Strategic Agility for a Faster-Moving World.* Boston: Harvard Business Review Press.

15. Lencioni, P. (2007). *The Five Dysfunctions of a Team: Team Assessment*. San Francisco: Pfeiffer.

16. McRaney, D. (2012). *You Are Not So Smart: Why You Have Too Many Friends on Facebook, Why Your Memory Is Mostly Fiction, and 46 Other Ways You're Deluding Yourself*. New York: Avery.

17. Patterson, K., Grenny, J., McMillan, R., & Switzler, A. (2012). *Crucial Conversations: Tools for Talking When Stakes Are High*. Singapore: McGraw-Hill Education.

18. Sutton, R. I. (2010). *The No Asshole Rule: Building a Civilized Workplace and Surviving One That Isn't*. New York: Business Plus.

ABOUT THE AUTHOR

———

Chris has over thirty years of helping clients succeed by helping them create world-class R&D teams. Chris's passion is helping teams transform to a much greater sense of purpose while creating dramatically greater value.

Over his career he has used his consulting skills to help his clients realize billions of dollars in returns through high-integrity R&D programs designed to reduce costs and reposition them in the market. During his career he has helped customers big and small solve tough problems in a variety of different industries including defense, property and casualty insurance, healthcare (both payer and provider, including children's hospitals), options trading, mortgages, IT outsourcing, the energy sector, mergers & acquisitions, IoT, and corporate technology strategy.

Chris's extensive career in technology R&D has enabled

him to help clients capitalize on trends often hidden by the froth of rapid change. His lifelong passion for helping teams succeed has resulted in a rich portfolio of proven best practices on building vibrant, engaged, high-performing teams. He also shares his experience through regular blogs he writes for thousands of followers in social media. Despite his early start in 1979, he is well versed in contemporary technologies like elastic infrastructure, development methodologies, and still writes production code in multiple languages as diverse as Python, Golang, Scala, and C++.

Before Adaptive, Chris helped create R&D teams with Cotiviti, iHealth Technologies, DST, CSC, Perot System, Hewlett Packard, and then for his own company, which he started in 1986. He's won nine patents for his clients and submitted an additional twelve applications. His research has led to numerous awards, including the HP Star Award, Perot Inventors Award, and in 1992 he won a fellowship from the National Institutes of Health to pursue his PhD in computational neuroscience at Syracuse University for his proposal to use neural networks as an interface for an artificial arm. The university later donated his research to the Veterans Health Administration.

Made in the
USA
Middletown, DE